Tenaya Lake near Tuolumne Meadows

Day Hikes
on the
Pacific Crest
Trail

California

George & Patricia Semb

WILDERNESS PRESS
BERKELEY

FIRST EDITION May 2000

All maps by George Semb
Design by Margaret Copeland
Cover design by Jaan Hitt

Front cover: Tuolumne Meadows and River
Back cover: Rugged country near Mount Lassen

Library of Congress Card Number 00-035177
ISBN 0-89997-256-x

Manufactured in the United States of America

Published by: **Wilderness Press**
               1200 5th St.
               Berkeley, CA 94710
               Phone (800) 443-7227
               mail@wildernesspress.com

               Visit our web site at **www.wildernesspress.com**
               Contact us for a free catalog

Printed on recycled paper, 20% post-consumer waste

Library of Congress Cataloging-in-Publication Data
Semb, George, 1943-
    Day hikes on the Pacific Crest Trail : California / George & Patricia
Semb.-- 1st ed.
        p. cm.
    Includes bibliographical references (p.) and index.
    ISBN 0-89997-256-X (alk. paper)
      1. Hiking--California--Guidebooks. 2. Hiking--Pacific Crest Trail--
Guidebooks. 3. California--Guidebooks. 4. Pacific Crest Trail--
Guidebooks. I. Semb, Patricia, 1956- II. Title.

GV199.42.C2 S46 2000
796.51'09794--dc21   00-035177

CONTENTS

ACKNOWLEDGEMENTS

We would like to thank several people who have helped us complete this project. Bob and Jackie Getty provided a base and a home for our car in Eugene, Oregon when we first began to day hike the PCT in 1996. Our friends Ed and Morgan Stephenson provided a base, and again a home for our car, in Snoqualmie Pass, Washington as we day hiked and mapped the PCT in Washington state. Another friend, Bob Peterson of Reno, did the same for us as we mapped and hiked in central and northern California. Mel Hovell and Carrie Cauchi, friends who live in San Diego, also opened their home and driveway as we mapped and hiked in southern California. We would also like to thank our editor, Thomas Winnett, whose meticulous attention to detail helped shape the final product. Finally, we cannot forget Rose Walkowicz, whose loving care kept our two geriatric cats, Sebastian and Beethoven, happy and content as their parents kept leaving home to gallivant in the west.

Preface

Introduction

My fascination with the Pacific Crest Trail began in 1976 while I was teaching at Georgetown University in Washington, D. C. One of my students mentioned that I had become more rotund since the semester had begun. Being a scientist and an observer of human behavior, I looked in the mirror to see if he was right. "Oh," I said to myself, "I am not rotund. I am fat."

From that day forward, I decided to do something I had never done in my life: exercise. So, for the next six months, I walked all over Washington, D.C. I walked to work every day from my apartment in Roslyn, over the Potomac River, to my office at Georgetown. I walked to the Kennedy Center every Thursday at noon to listen to organ recitals. One day I walked to the National Geographic Society Headquarters, where I bought a book entitled *The Pacific Crest Trail* by William R. Gray (1975).

The scenery in the photographs was stunning. The text itself was interesting, but appeared to have been written for mountain climbers and long-distance backpackers. I did not include myself, nor did I envision myself, in either of those categories. But I did make a mental note to someday to travel in the West to see the beautiful land through which the Pacific Crest Trail passes.

Mental notes often lie dormant for years. In this case, it was 17 years. In the interim, I ended my year at Georgetown and returned to the University of Kansas in Lawrence where I have taught—and continue to do so—since 1972. In 1983, I met Patricia and we were married the following year. During the next few years, I made many trips to the West Coast to work for the Department of the Navy in Monterey and San Diego, and to visit friends who lived in Eugene and Seattle. So, the stage was "set" so to speak for us to "discover" the PCT.

In 1993, we went to Seattle to visit Ed and Beth Stephenson. Some years before, they had moved from the hustle and bustle of the "city" to the small community—and we emphasize the term community because

Authors at the south Terminus near the Mexican border

it really is one—of Snoqualmie Pass. Pat went on her first backpacking trip, from Tucquala Meadows to Peggy's Pond behind Cathedral Rock. We did day hikes to Deep Lake and to Deception Pass. One of the signs along the way identified the trail we were on as the Pacific Crest Trail (PCT). When we returned to Ed and Beth's home at Snoqualmie Pass, we noticed the PCT trailhead sign on Alpental road. The mental note I had made 17 years earlier resurfaced, and when we returned home to Kansas, I looked once again at Gray's *Pacific Crest Trail*. I made another mental note to find out more about the PCT.

Two years passed and in May 1995 Pat and I went to an orienteering meet in the Laguna Mountains near San Diego. As we were navigating through the woods, we kept crossing the PCT. "This is the same trail," I said to Pat, "that passes right by Ed and Beth's house at Snoqualmie Pass. I made another mental note to look into the PCT when we got home.

This time the mental note was warm, and in early in 1996 we purchased

The Pacific Crest Trail, Volume 1: California by Jeffrey P. Schaffer, Ben Schifrin, Thomas Winnett, and Ruby Johnson Jenkins (1995) and *The Pacific Crest Trail, Volume 2: Oregon and Washington* by Jeffrey P. Schaffer and Andy Selters (1992) in a retail store in Overland Park, KS. The clerk was happy that someone had finally purchased copies of this West Coast guide.

As we started to read, we realized just how mammoth this trail is, not to mention the incredible amount of time and effort that the authors had put into creating such a detailed, comprehensive guide. "Maybe," we thought, "just maybe, we can hike part of it. Next time we go to San Diego we'll take a look." That day came a few weeks later during Spring Break when we went to the South Terminus at the Mexican border and hiked 2.3 miles to Highway 94. Three days later, we trekked 17.2 miles from Moreno Lake through Hauser Canyon to Highway 94. The PCT journey had begun.

We spent the following summer, still 1996, in Oregon. We did several day hikes in Section B (I-5 near Siskiyou Pass to Highway 140 near Fish Lake) and Section C (Highway 140 to Highway 138 near Crater Lake National Park). One of those hikes dealt us a healthy dose of reality. We started the day at Sevenmile Marsh Trailhead and hiked together six miles into Sky Lakes Wilderness. Pat turned around to go back to the car to drive to the Cold Springs trailhead. From there, she would hike in to meet me and we would hike out together. (This is one of the hiking scenarios we describe at the end of this Preface.) Imagine Pat's growing concern when she did not meet me on the trail. She walked back to the Cold Springs trailhead and waited until 5:30, by which time I surely should have reached there. So, the emergency plan we had made earlier in the day went into effect: Pat immediately drove back toward the Sevenmile Marsh trailhead, where we had begun the day's hike.

As much as we both love the outdoors, we also know there are risks in outings like these. A primary objective is to limit those risks. We cannot emphasize enough that you must know the limits of your endurance, both mental and physical, and that you exercise caution, particularly when you are fatigued.

On this particular day, I made some foolish decisions as I approached the Devils Peak/Lee Peak Saddle (7,320). I was hiking from north to south, so I could see the wall of snow facing me as I started up toward the saddle. Many hikers coming from the south slide down these snowfields. However, this can be risky if you are not experienced in dealing with snowfields. You must pay attention to what you're sliding into. If you end up in rocks or encounter a tree on the way down, serious injury or even death may result. Needless-to-say, I did not have any experience with snowfields, nor did I have, or know how to use, an ice axe.

I had been climbing the snowfield for several hundred feet as I neared the saddle. I could see tracks in the snow in front of me, but I did not realize just how steep the ascent had become. I lost my footing and slid several hundred feet, hitting small trees, roots, and rocks along the way. Luckily, I only scrapped arms and elbows and bruised ribs. Despite losing all but one water bottle, I was able to walk out. During that hike—7.5 miles to the Sevenmile Marsh trailhead, then 5.7 miles down the access road—I did not meet another soul. At about 6:30 Pat spotted me along the Sevenmile Marsh trailhead access road. She was relieved that my injuries were not too serious, and I was happy to put that day behind us.

That incident reinforced several important points. First, always establish one or more emergency plans—we'll have more to say about the specifics of those later. Second, when an emergency arises, follow the plan. The reason you make a plan is to have a set of procedures to follow when and if an emergency occurs.

The other thing the incident did was to get us to re-think what kind of hikes we were going to do. We were using these day hikes to build up to longer backpacking expeditions along the trail. We had all of our backpacking gear with us, but I knew it was going to take a few days to recover from my fall. We also agreed that we liked doing day hikes. Much as we enjoyed backpacking, these day hikes were appealing, and what the heck, we had already day-hiked from the California-Oregon border to the entrance to Crater Lake National Park. We wondered just how much trail we could day-hike. At the same time, just for fun, we started to chronicle these day hikes. By the end of the fall, we had day hiked every single mile of the 464.6 PCT miles in Oregon, from Wards Fork Gap just south of the Oregon border to the Bridge of the Gods at the Columbia River.

Next, we explored Washington and mapped out 18 day hikes covering some 246.1 miles between the Bridge of the Gods and Highway I-90 at Snoqualmie Pass. The northern 261.1 PCT miles in Washington, from I-90 at Snoqualmie Pass to Manning Park just north of the Canadian border appeared more challenging for day hikers. However, we mapped out 13 day hikes that covered 135.6 of those miles.

Miles You Can Day Hike on the PCT

Overall, of the 1,006.2 PCT miles between Seiad Valley near the Oregon-California border and Manning Park north of the Canadian border, 879.4 (87%) are accessible to day hikers. These day hikes have a total mileage themselves of 1057.0 miles. Thus, to hike these 879.4 PCT miles, it will "cost" you 177.6 additional miles to access the PCT from trailheads along the way. In all, we describe 71 day hikes in Oregon and Washington, from Seiad Valley in northern California to Manning Park

Tuolumne Meadows and River

just north of the Canadian border. (To be consistent with the Sections in the Schaffer guides, we include two hikes in northern California in the Oregon-Washington guide and two hikes in southern Oregon in the California guide.)

Given our successes with identifying day hikes along the PCT in Oregon and Washington, we turned our attention to California. In 1998, we visited Southern California and discovered that you can day-hike 563.7 PCT miles from the Mexican border to Highway 58 near Tehachapi Pass. Later that summer, we identified day hikes in Northern California and Southern Oregon that covered over 700 miles from Sonora Pass near Lake Tahoe to the California-Oregon border. Overall, we have identified day hikes that cover 1,491.0 (86%) of the 1,732.2 PCT miles in California and Southern Oregon. These day hikes have a total mileage themselves of 1,663.3 miles. Thus, to hike 1491.0 miles on the PCT in California and Southern Oregon, it will "cost" you 172.3 miles to access the PCT from trailheads along the way. In all, we describe 124 day hikes from the Mexican border to I-5 near Siskiyou Pass in southern Oregon.

The only part of California that is not readily accessible to day hikers is the High Sierra from south of Mt. Whitney to Sonora Pass north of Yosemite National Park. Although day hikers can access stretches of the PCT in this region, hikes along the trail are limited. Furthermore, hiking in this area is challenging because (1) the altitude mostly exceeds 10,000 feet, (2) the terrain is steep, and (3) there are several treacherous river crossings. These are all factors that must be considered when hiking in the mountains, and these are mountains.

Conventions

This guide contains 18 sections (A-R) in the California edition and 12 sections (A-L) in the Oregon-Washington edition. These sections correspond exactly to the sections described in the Schaffer guides for California and for Oregon-Washington. While the Schaffer guides concentrate more on the trail and how to hike it step-by-step, our guides concentrate more on how to reach the various trailheads that take you to the PCT.

The official name for the PCT is the Pacific Crest National Scenic Trail, a name you will see on Forest Service maps. It is also designated as Trail 2000. One of the U.S. Government agencies you will surely encounter along the way is the United States Forest Service (USFS). We have met and interacted with hundreds of dedicated, helpful employees. We always try to go out of our way to tell rangers and other personnel how much we appreciate their help.

For each of these day hikes on the PCT, we include several pieces of information. First, within each Section, the hikes are numbered sequentially. Second, we name the starting point (Stephenson Peak Road) and the stopping point (Lucky 5 Ranch Gate on Highway S1). Third, we tell you how far you will hike on the PCT, and fourth, the total distance of the hike if the trailhead is not located directly on the PCT. Fifth, we refer you to the corresponding USFS map (Map: A-5 (Cleveland NF)). Sixth, we rate the difficulty of the hike (Easy, Moderate, Difficult) These ratings are based on mile and elevation change, with shorter (less than 10 miles), more level hikes rated as easy and longer (more than 20 miles), steeper hikes rated as difficult. Seventh, we recommend the direction you should do the hike.

Similar to the Schaffer guides, we describe each day hike from south to north. We did not do all of the individual hikes from south to north, but like Schaffer, we journal them that way. When it made sense to go in the opposite direction (N→S), we give our reason for doing so, such as elevation change, ease of access to the trail, lingering snow, river crossings, or other risk factors. Our goal is to make one of America's premiere trails accessible to many day hikers who might have otherwise considered it inaccessible. Proceeding one day at a time, we have now made an impressive dent in the map on our wall that stretches from the Mexican border to Manning Park just north of the Canadian border.

Next, we briefly describe each hike, paying particular attention to major features along the way, as well as any risks that may be involved. These descriptions are not nearly as complete as you will find in the

Schaffer guides, and we highly recommend that you use the Schaffer guides for their detailed description of the trail itself.

In writing this guide, we were faced with the problem of balancing the amount of space we devoted to describing each day hike and the amount of space telling you how to find the trailheads. Given the rich descriptions of the PCT itself in the Schaffer guides, we concentrated more on making certain that you can locate the PCT. After all, if you cannot find the PCT, you are not going to be able to do day hikes on it. Thus, we include highly detailed directions on how to get to and from trailheads on or that lead to the PCT, including road names, road numbers, the direction you should turn at each intersection, and the distance you should travel on each road measured in tenths of a mile. Finally, we identify a few places to stay and to eat along the way.

Maps

We use Forest Service (USFS) maps to show the day hikes, access trails, and access roads in this guide. There are several reasons for this. First, all of the topographic maps we inspected suffer from what we call a "size" problem. The ones with the greatest clarity are just too big to fit on a single or a double page. For most of the hikes, the roads that you need to follow to reach the PCT would take three or four pages of maps to show the entire picture. Even then, the picture would not be very clear because one map would be on several pages. Second, when we inspected smaller-scale topographic maps, we found that many of the roads and landmarks were not well enough represented to give you the detailed instructions that you would need to find the PCT, the access trails, and the access roads. Nevertheless, we highly recommend that you use these maps in conjunction with the more detailed topographic maps found in the Schaffer guides. The Schaffer guides provide much more detail in both maps and hike descriptions than we could provide here.

USFS maps cover nearly all of the PCT from Mexico to Canada. Furthermore, they depict both the trail and the access trails/roads that lead to it. While lacking topographic detail, they provide an amazingly accurate representation of the roads and trails that surround and include the PCT. Furthermore, their scale (1:126,720) allows a view of the "context," the surrounding country side. You can visualize where you are in relation to the surrounding area. We have used these maps to find every single one of the trailheads identified in this guide, and we have used them to do many of the day hikes we describe.

Every hike has a corresponding map. Most of the hikes require only one map, but a few cover enough territory to require two, or in one instance three, maps. We have tried to include enough detail on the maps and in the text so that you can navigate to each trailhead. We frequently note at the top, bottom or side of a map what other map to look at for a continuation of the land.

Almost all of the maps in this guide are oriented with north at the top of the page. A few maps are too wide for that, so you have to rotate the book 90° to view the map. For these maps we have included a north arrow on the page. Rather than show declination on each map, we include it at the beginning of each section. As a general rule, if you use 15° as the difference between magnetic north (what your compass shows) and true north (what the maps show), you will be very close to the average declination along the PCT. For example, declination is 13° east near the Mexican border, then increases gradually as you work your way north to near the Canadian border, where it is 20° east.

There are several other conventions we use. First, each trailhead is shown as a distinct dot on the map. Second, we depict the PCT as a solid black line. On some maps, you will see another dark line in the vicinity of the PCT. The other line is usually a county line which tends to follow the actual crest closely, with one county to the east and the other to the west. You can tell the difference between two lines by using the trailhead dots to identify the PCT. Third, we depict access trails that take you from the trailhead to the PCT as white lines. Fourth, we use a solid gray line to identify the access roads you follow to reach the trailheads. We also identify these roads by name, such as Hwy I-5, Hwy 12, Hwy 138, Hwy N2, FR 24, FR 43N44, or FR 120. Furthermore, when there is a road junction in the text, we mark it with an "X" on the map. Finally, "TH" in the text means trailhead, "CG" means campground, "TC" means trail camp, and "TT" means truck trail.

Roads and Cars

It would be nice if all the roads that lead to the PCT and trails that take you to it were paved. As many Forest Service maps proclaim, "getting around on National Forest Roads is different from driving on a city street or State highway." That is an understatement.

It will help you greatly if you learn how to read the US Forest Service maps we include in this guide, together with the nomenclature that the USFS uses. The legend here should help you in that endeavor. Throughout this guide, we use the letters FR to represent Forest Roads. There are several different types of FRs. First, there are single- or double-digit FRs, such as FR 3 and FR 24. The USFS defines these as "primary" routes. Second, there are four-digit FRs such as FR 23N27 and FR 2000. The USFS calls these "secondary" routes. Third, there are three-digit roads such as FR 120, which may or may not be maintained on a regular basis by the USFS. In general, primary roads are better than secondary roads, and secondary roads are better than those that may or may not be maintained. However, there are exceptions to every rule, and we have found more than our fair share of primary roads that are rougher than nearby secondary roads. We have also found some very good three-digit roads as well as some three-digit roads that you could not travel even with a "four-wheel drive" (4WD). Fortunately, for you, our readers, we have traveled all of these roads and provide enough detail so that you will know what to expect.

Another note about roads: If two numbered roads are on the same path at the point in question, we say, for example, Highway 36/89. If we are at a junction of two, we say Highways 36/89.

In preparing this guide, we have analyzed several ways to get from Point A to Point B. Often, the map suggested a road that might work, but when we field-checked it, it did not. We want to state from the outset that we have checked all of the roads to all of the trailheads we describe in this guide. Furthermore, when we say that you can get to a trailhead by passenger car, we have in fact driven there in a passenger car. When we say that a road is 4WD only, we mean it.

Throughout this guide, you can assume that a road is paved unless we tell you otherwise. When pavement surfaces vary, we tell you which roads are paved and which roads are dirt. We also point out when a road turns from paved to dirt, or vice versa, to help you mark your progress along the route we have described. Furthermore, we discriminate between good dirt roads and rough dirt roads. You can assume that a dirt road is good unless we identify it as a rough dirt road. What, exactly, is a rough dirt road? It is a road that you might feel more comfortable traversing in a high-clearance 4WD, but that you can navigate if you drive slowly and cautiously. You may have to drive around deep depressions or even stop and move rocks that look too large to drive over. Some of these roads can be quite steep, while others have deep ruts. We want to reiterate that we have driven every single rough road in this guide in a passenger car. Those cars included a 1987 Acura Legend, a 1997 Ford Contour, a 1998 Toyota Corolla, and a 1997 Toyota Camry, to name a few. We have broken one oil pan and one clutch. We categorized the roads on which these incidents occurred as 4WD only. We have also experienced scratches, minor dents, and flat tires. Clearly, we do not recommend that you take your brand new Viper or Lexus on any of these rough dirt roads, but we do not want to discourage you from using whatever vehicle you feel comfortable with to get to these trailheads.

National Forests Along the Way, from S→N

Cleveland National Forest
10845 Rancho Bernardo Rd.,
  Suite 200
Rancho Bernardo, CA 92127-2107
(619) 673-6180

San Bernardino National Forest
1824 South Commercenter Circle
San Bernardino, CA 92408-3430
(909) 383-5588

Angeles National Forest
701 North Santa Anita Avenue
Arcadia, CA 91006
(626) 574-1613

Sequoia National Forest
900 West Grand Avenue
Porterville, CA 93257
(559) 784-1500

Inyo National Forest
873 North Main Street
Bishop, CA 93514
(760) 873-2400

Sierra National Forest
1600 Tollhouse Road
Clovis, CA 93612
(559) 297-0706

Stanislaus National Forest
19777 Greenley Road
Sonora, CA 95370
(209) 532-3671

Eldorado National Forest
100 Forni Road
Placerville, CA 95667
(530) 622-5061

Tahoe National Forest
631 Coyote Street
Nevada City, CA 95959
(530) 265-4531

Plumas National Forest
159 Lawrence Street
Quincy, CA 95971
(530) 283-2050

Lassen National Forest
55 South Sacramento Street
Susanville, CA 96130
(530) 257-2151

Shasta-Trinity National Forest
2400 Washington Avenue
Redding, CA 96001
(530) 244-2978

Klamath National Forest
1312 Fairlane Road
Yreka, CA 96097
(530) 842-6131

Rogue River National Forest
333 West 8th Street
Medford, OR 97501
(541) 858-2200

Mountains in Castle Crags State Park

Pacific Crest Trail Association

We enthusiastically endorse this association. Its mission is to "promote and protect the Pacific Crest National Scenic Trail so as to reflect its world-class significance for the enjoyment, education and adventure of hikers and equestrians." The association publishes the "Pacific Crest Trail Communicator" six times a year, an informative magazine with letters, news, features, and photographs related to the PCT. It also coordinates volunteer projects and sponsors gatherings and meetings. Perhaps its most important function, however, is to maintain a website (www.pcta.org) that provides timely updates to trail conditions throughout the hiking season. This comprehensive website is a "must-read" for day hikers and long-distance trekkers alike. Memberships rates begin at just $35 per year. You can write them at 5325 Elkhorn Blvd. No. 256, Sacramento, CA 95842-2526, phone them at (916) 349-2109, or e-mail them at info@pcta.org.

Cost

Coincidentally, one thing that has made this endeavor possible was a stock we owned, Property Capital Trust, whose ticker symbol was PCT. We're not kidding. We eventually sold the stock and used some of the proceeds to fund our adventure—which brings us to the subject of cost. Most PCT guidebooks are written for (1) people on a strict budget and (2) those who backpack long parts of the trail. Make no mistake, we love to backpack, but as we get older, we realize that 100-mile treks in the high country push us to our limits.

What we did here is more expensive and less demanding. Because these are day hikes, there is no need to carry a backpack. Again, make no mistake, we still carry a day pack that contains all of our emergency gear. Sometimes, we camp near or at one of the trailheads. Other times, we stay in motels or bed and breakfast inns. Sometimes, we use two cars. All of these add to the expense, but they also reduce the risks, thus enabling us to accomplish our long-term goal of hiking most of the PCT.

Hiking Scenarios

Scenario 1: *Hike Together at the Beginning and at the End.* On some days, we would start at the same point and hike together two or three miles (or hours), at which point one of us would turn around and trek back to the starting point. The other person would continue on to the end point. Thus, one of us would complete the entire segment. The other person moves the car to the end point, and then hikes back on the trail to meet the "hiker." Thus, while one of us missed part of the adventure for the day, at least one us walked every mile of the segment. This scenario suffers from an obvious drawback: the "hiker" is by him or herself for at least half of the hike. It also involves risks.

The Devils Peak/Lee Peak Saddle incident we described earlier, in which one of us fell down a snowfield and had to walk several miles to the trailhead, reinforced several important points. First, always establish a time when the driver will leave the end point and return to the starting point. When the established time arrived for Pat, she returned immediately to the starting point, where she found me sitting at the TH. The law for the "driver" is: when the established time arrives, and the "hiker" isn't there, return by the same route used from the starting point to the end point. We always allow for a large margin of error in establishing the time by which we should meet. When that margin of error is exceeded, and the hiker hasn't arrived, the driver heads back. The law for the "hiker" is: if there is a problem, return to the starting point on exactly the same route you hiked away from it on. An injured hiker should stay on the original route, to make it easier for search and rescue to find him/her. We cannot overemphasize the need to establish rules and times, and to follow those rules until the missing hiker is found or is reported as "lost" to the authorities.

Suppose the driver returns to the starting point but does not find the missing hiker. At this point, the driver should alert the authorities, then return to the end point to check one more time for the missing hiker.

Clearly, with more people, other contingency plans can be arranged that may increase the margin of safety for everyone involved.

Scenario 2: *Hike alone, Meet in the Middle.* In this scenario, one person drops the other at the starting point, then immediately drives the car to the end point. Both people hike toward the other and meet near the middle. Then both continue to their destinations. The hiker who arrives at the car drives back to the starting point to retrieve the other person. This allows both people to hike the entire segment of the trail. The obvious drawback is that each person hikes alone for all of the day. Some of you may consider this scenario too lonely or too risky.

As with the first scenario, you always need to have an emergency contingency plan, and stick to it. When we both hike alone and meet in the middle, we establish a time by which we should meet. When we establish that time, we allow for a comfortable margin of error. If we do not meet by that time, each returns to his/her original starting point by exactly their same route. After we return to our respective starting points, the person with the car drives back to the original starting point. Thus, if there is a problem, we know where to search for the other person. Of course, there are risks associated with this scenario, too, the most obvious of which is: if the person who is to drive the car is injured, the other person is left at the other TH without a car.

The second thing we learned from the Devils Peak/Lee Peak Saddle incident described earlier is that for us, both of these scenarios may be too risky, particularly where there are significant snowfields or dangerous rivers to ford, in which case we may postpone the hike to a later time. These are factors you will have to address as well, and we encourage you to address them early in your planning process.

Being able to communicate with one another while hiking alone would certainly reduce the risk. We tried cellular phones in Oregon. However, because the PCT is located in some of the most remote parts of the state, they did not work. We are confident that by the time you read this, cellular communication will be possible along the trail. As a backup and for emergencies, it is essential.

Scenario 3: *Two Cars (the More, the Merrier).* Having two cars is more expensive, but it reduces the risk and enhances the enjoyment. Furthermore, the more people you hike with, the better. Whenever possible, we have teamed up with other hikers. The problem is finding others who have similar goals and endurance.

With two cars, you have several options. One is similar to Scenario 2, in which one person (group) starts at one end of the hike and the other person (group) starts at the opposite end. You meet in the middle and hike out separately, but unlike in Scenario 2, both exiting parties have cars waiting for them. The major disadvantage is that the two people (or groups) hike by themselves for all of the day. Another option is to leave one car at TH A, then transport everyone in the other car to TH B. Everyone hikes together to TH A, and at the end of the day, everyone returns to TH B.

Scenario 4: *Hike in and out on the same Route.* This is such an obvious strategy that we almost forgot to describe it. If one of the other scenarios presents too much risk or difficulty, consider hiking in and out on the same route. This enables all parties to hike together and eliminates much of the planning associated with the other scenarios. The obvious disadvantage is that you may cover less of the trail.

What to Take on a Day Hike

We believe strongly in checklists. They help you prepare for your day hike by reminding you in a very concrete way exactly what you need to take with you. There are several very good day-hike/backpack books that detail all kinds of useful information for excursions into the back country. We recommend *The Complete Walker III* by Colin Fletcher (1996), and, of course, the two Schaffer Pacific Crest Trail guides.

Here is what we carry when we hike on the PCT. It can serve as a starting list for what you may want to take along. Before you head out, however, please spend some time in the library on the world-wide web researching the latest recommendations for what you should carry with you.

Day Pack
   First Aid Kit: bandages, gauze, blister kit, Neosporin, scissors,
   Imodium
   Compass
   Maps
   Fire-starter kit (must be kept dry)
      Matches in water-tight case or butane lighter
   Birthday candle and dry tinder
   Gore-Tex jacket
   Mittens
   Wool cap
   Whistle
   Gore-Tex or nylon pants
   Plastic garbage bag—33 gallon (waterproof liner and potential rain
      shield)
   Space blanket
   Insect repellent

Sun hat
Head lamp with new batteries
Toilet paper
Trowel
Resealable plastic bag for money, driver's license, credit card
Water (minimum 1 pint for every 2 hours or 4 miles)
Water purifier or iodine pills
Buck knife/Swiss Army knife
Duck tape
Sunscreen
Food—whatever you like, but not too much.
Any prescription drugs

Other Items
Walking stick(s)
Camera: extra film and back-up batteries
Ice axe
Crampons
Tennis shoes, sandals, or water shoes for river/creek crossings

What to Wear—depends on temperature
T-shirt or Capilene shirt
Breathable jacket/shell (e.g., Patagonia)
Underwear
Hiking pants/shorts
Sweat band or bandana
Socks
Hiking boots or tennis shoes

Feedback

We have tried to be as complete and accurate as we could in preparing this guide, but we realize there will be errors. When you find an error, or something that could be improved, please let us know, at Wilderness Press, 1200 5th St., Berkeley, CA 94710 or via e-mail at www.wilderness-press.com. We also plan to provide you with a way to check and file road and trail reports in California through our website, www.semb.com, which we will update on a regular basis.

LEGEND

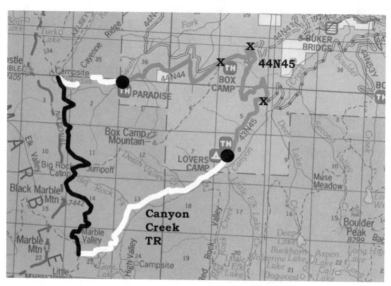

Sample Map

On all of our maps:

● = Trailhead

Solid, black line = PCT

White line = Access trail

Solid, gray line = Access road

X = Significant road junction

44N44 = Forest Road

On some maps:

Solid black/gray line = County line or
    National Forest boundary

Dashed gray line = County line

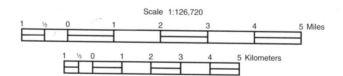

Mexican Border to Warner Springs

Overview

PCT: 110.6 miles
Day Hikes (8): 112.2 miles
Declination: 13° E

From the South Terminus (2915), the PCT leads north through near-desert terrain, then climbs several thousand feet into the Laguna Mountains. From there, you hike along a ridge with spectacular views of the desert floor 4000 feet below, then descend into San Felipe Valley (2252). You make a moderate climb to a ridge in the San Felipe Hills, then undulate along until reaching a sweeping valley and the ranch called Warner Springs (3040).

Hike 1—Mexican Border to Highway 94

PCT: 2.3 miles
Hike: 2.3 miles
Map: A-1 (Cleveland NF)
Difficulty: Easy

Hike. We stopped at the Campo Border Patrol office to see if they had had any reports of problems in the area. They had not. We recommend you do the same as a safety precaution. Next, we drove to the Mexican border and the Southern Terminus to take photographs. It is a desolate place, but that is how the desert is supposed to be.

Proceeding N 1.3 miles from the Southern Terminus (2915), the PCT parallels the same roads you will follow to reach it. Then, you turn west and follow a bushy slope 1.0 mile to Highway 94—Campo Highway (2475).

Mexican Border. Take the Buckman Springs exit off I-8 (see Map A-3). Go W 0.1 mile to Highway S1. Turn left (S) and go 10.0 miles to

**For roads from I-8,
see maps A-2 and A-3**

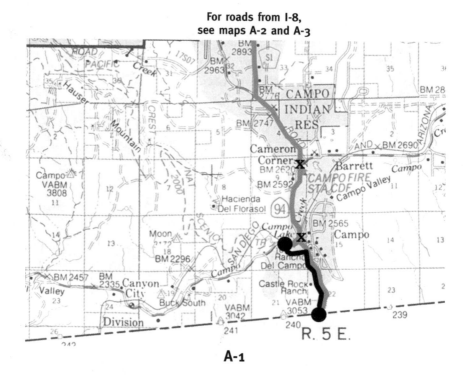

A-1

Highway 94 (see Map A-2). Turn right (SW) and go 1.5 miles to Forrest Gate road, just west of Campo Creek. There is a market on the north side of the road. Turn left (S) on Forrest Gate road and go 0.6 mile, past the Border Patrol Station and the Juvenile Ranch Facility, until the pavement ends. Continue straight (S) 0.2 mile on the dirt road, then jog left (E) 0.1 mile. Now turn right (S) and go 0.5 mile, under some power lines, to the junction of several roads. You can see the terminus 0.1 mile to the SE. Take any of the roads that lead in that direction. The terminus sits on a hill in front of the fence that separates Mexico and the United States. (From just south of the Border Patrol Station, the roads described here parallel the PCT.)

🚐 **Highway 94.** Retrace your route from the terminus to the junction of Highway 94 and Forrest Gate road in Campo. Turn left (W) on Highway 94 and go 0.5 mile to the PCT, just west of Milepost 50.00. There are PCT signs on both sides of the road. Parking along Highway 94 is limited, but you can park along the paved road that goes north from Highway 94 just before you cross the PCT.

Hike 2—Highway 94 to Lake Morena County Park

PCT: 17.9 miles
Hike: 17.9 miles
Map: A-2 (Cleveland NF)
Difficulty: Moderate

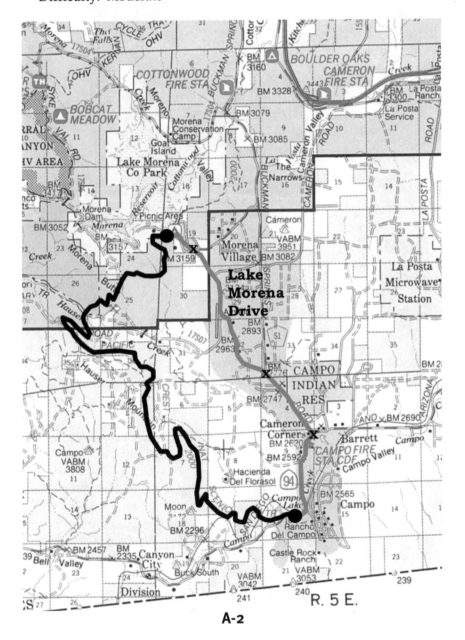

A-2

Lake Morena as seen from the PCT near Kitchen Creek Road

Hike. Hauser Wilderness and Hauser Canyon are spectacular, and this is only the beginning of the PCT! When we hiked it in March, we saw a lot of wildlife, but no people.

From Highway 94 (2475), you hike west across abandoned railroad tracks before climbing north past Hauser Mountain, a total of 9.2 miles. You descend along the north face of Hauser Mountain 2.7 miles to South Boundary road (2910), which you follow down 0.8 mile to a trail that leads another 0.7 mile to Hauser Canyon road (2320). You then hike up the other side of the canyon before making a moderate descent to Lake Morena County Park (3065). The final leg, from Hauser Creek to Lake Morena County Park, is 4.5 miles.

Dining tip. At the end of the trek, we stopped at the Oak Shores Store in Lake Morena for an old-fashioned malt, one made with real ice cream and whole milk, a nice reward after a long day.

Lake Morena County Park from Campo to the south. Return to the junction of Highway 94 and Forrest Gate road in Campo. Turn left (N) on Highway 94 and go 1.5 miles to Highway S1 (Buckman Springs road). Turn left (NW) on S1 and go 1.5 miles to Lake Morena Drive. Bear left (NW) and go 3.0 miles to the junction of Lake Morena Drive and Oak Drive. Bear left (NW) on Lake Morena Drive and go 0.4 mile to Lake Morena County Park. There is a parking area on the south side of the road just before you enter the County Park at the intersection of Lake Morena Drive and Lake Shore Drive.

🚐 **Lake Morena County Park from Highway I-8 to the north**. Take the Buckman Springs exit off I-8 (see Map A-3). Go W 0.1 mile to Highway S1. Turn left (S) and go 5.3 miles to Oak Drive. Bear right (SW) on Oak Drive and go 1.5 mile to Lake Morena Drive. Turn right (NW) on Lake Morena Drive and go 0.4 mile to the County Park.

Hike 3—Lake Morena County Park to Cibbets Flat CG

PCT: 12.6 miles
Hike: 13.4 miles
Map: A-3 (Cleveland NF)
Difficulty: Moderate
Direction: N→S (Elevation)

🎒 **Hike.** We did this hike N→S because of the elevation change, from 3065 feet at Lake Morena County Park to 4410 feet at Fred Canyon road. This is not a huge climb, but when we have a choice, we sometimes prefer down to up. However, to be consistent with the flow of the trail, we describe the hike S→N.

From the entrance to Lake Morena County Park (3065), hike north on Lake Shore Drive. PCT signs on the telephone poles mark the way. In about 200 yards (0.1 mile) a sign directs you to the PCT. In 4.0 miles you reach Cottonwood Creek (3065), and in another 1.8 miles the Boulder Oaks CG (3170). Walk another 0.4 mile through the CG to Boulder Oaks Store (3150). Immediately across the road is the PCT TH. From here, you hike 3.8 miles, passing under Highway I-8 and up to a crossing of Kitchen Creek road (3990). (If you turn around, you can see Highway I-8 and Lake Morena in the distance. It is nice to be able to see where you have been, and where you are going. Such vistas are common along the PCT.) Continue 2.5 miles into Fred Canyon to Fred Canyon Road 16S08 (4410). Hike 0.8 mile down Fred Canyon Road 16S08 to the Cibbets Flat CG.

🚐 **Cibbets Flat CG**. Retrace your route to Highway I-8. Go east on Highway I-8 to Cameron Station/Kitchen Creek road exit. Go north on paved Kitchen Creek road. You cross the PCT 2.5 miles north of the exit. Continue another 2.2 miles to the Cibbets Flat CG access road. Turn right (E) and follow the access road 0.2 mile to the CG and Fred Canyon Road 16S08. You can park outside the CG along Fred Canyon road.

As you enter National Forest land at the Cameron Fire Station, a sign greets you, PARKED VEHICLES MUST DISPLAY A FOREST ADVENTURE PASS. This is the latest "tax" the US Forest Service imposes on us "adventurers" (users). It costs $5 a day, or $30 for an annual pass. This pass covers, S→N, Cleveland, San Bernardino, Angeles, and Los Padres National Forests.

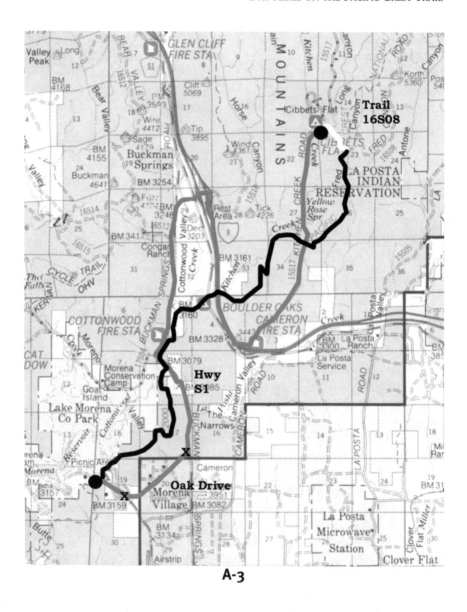

A-3

For an extra $5, you can get a permit for a second car, but the second permit can be obtained only from a District Office. Day and single-vehicle passes are available at ranger stations, gas stations, and places that sell outdoor gear (e.g., REI and Adventure 16). The fine for not displaying a pass in required areas is $100. According to the brochure, 80% of the funds obtained from the passes—and from the fines, we assume—go back to the National Forest where the fee was collected.

Hike 4—Cibbets Flat CG to Stephenson Peak Road

PCT: 10.1 miles
Hike: 10.9 miles
Map: A-4 (Cleveland NF)
Difficulty: Moderate
Direction: N→S (Elevation)

🥾 **Hike.** We recommend this hike N→S because of the elevation change, from 5985 feet at Stephenson Peak road to 4410 feet in Fred Canyon. However, as usual, we describe it S→N. To begin, go E 0.8 mile up Fred Canyon Road 16S08 to the PCT (4410). From there, it is N 4.2 miles up Fred Canyon to Long Canyon (5230). A moderate 0.8 mile climb brings you to Long Canyon Creek (5435). Go N 2.3 miles to Morris Ranch road (6005). It is another 1.5 miles to the Burnt Rancheria CG boundary (5950). Pass through the CG and proceed 1.2 miles to Desert View Picnic Area and desert overlook. It is another 0.1 mile to Stephenson Peak road (5980).

🚐 **Stephenson Peak Road—preferred option.** From the Cibbets Flat CG, retrace your route S 4.7 miles to Highway I-8. Go W on Highway I-8 to Sunrise Highway S1. Go N 10.0 miles on Highway S1 to Desert View Overlook, where you can park and look at the desert floor 4400 feet below. Stephenson Peak road is 0.1 mile further north on Highway S1, but parking here is limited.

🚐 **Stephenson Peak Road—second option, sometimes.** From the entrance to the Cibbets Flat CG, go N 0.8 mile on Kitchen Creek road to a sign that reads END COUNTY MAINTENANCE and a gate with a sign that announces CLOSED SUNSET TO SUNRISE. Here the road becomes paved, one-lane FR 15S17. If the gate is open, you can continue N 6.3 miles to another gate and Sunrise Highway S1.

DAY HIKES
One beauty of day hikes is that parts of the PCT are accessible all year long. We did this particular hike on Christmas Eve day. There was some ice on the trail, primarily frozen puddles. Overall, it was a cool experience.

At the junction of Kitchen Creek road and Highway S1, you are 11.8 miles north of Highway I-8 and 3.1 miles south and east of Desert View Overlook. Sometimes, however, Kitchen Creek road is gated where it intersects Highway S1. It is very frustrating to drive Kitchen Creek road only to find that you cannot exit at Highway S1. It is even more frustrating to arrive at S1, then have to turn around, only to discover that the gate at

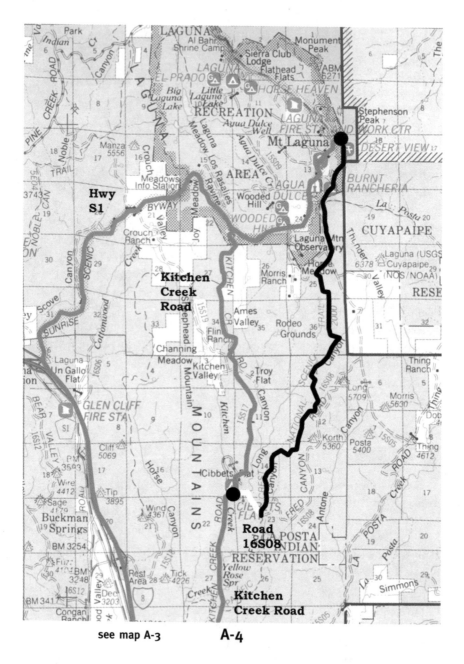

see map A-3   A-4

the other end has also been locked, and you can't get out, no matter which way you go. Why are the gates sometimes locked, and whom can you call to find out if they are? Unfortunately, two agencies, the USFS and the Border Patrol, have keys to these locks. Depending on the amount of illegal alien activity in the area, nobody knows when the gates will be locked.

PCT marker near Kitchen Creek Road with hiker on the PCT

Thus, the safest option from the Cibbets Flat CG to Stephenson Peak road is to retrace your route to I-8 and go west on Sunrise Highway S1.

Hike 5—Stephenson Peak Road to Lucky 5 Ranch Gate on Highway S1

PCT: 15.5 miles
Hike: 15.5 miles
Map: A-5 (Cleveland NF)
Difficulty: Moderate
Direction: N→S (Access)

Hike. Hiking north from Stephenson Peak road (5980), there are several great views of the desert floor below. In the next 10.1 miles, you cross several jeep roads, but you essentially parallel Sunrise Highway S1 before arriving at the Pioneer Mail Picnic Area and TH (5260). In 0.7 mile you cross paved Kwaaymii Point road (5450) and in another 1.4 miles a jeep road into Oriflamme Canyon (5250). You intersect a second jeep road

THE COMET HALE-BOPP

We did many of the Laguna day hikes during March, 1997, the same time the Comet Hale-Bopp made its debut. We watched in awe as Hale-Bopp crossed the sky, sky so dark and clear because we were 6000 feet above sea level and far away from city lights.

(4875) into Oriflamme Canyon 2.8 miles further. At this point, you need to pay careful attention to your map and the following directions. As the PCT swoops down to the jeep trail into Oriflamme Canyon to the east, it also intersects a north-south jeep trail. From there, there are two ways to reach the Lucky 5 Ranch gate on Highway S1.

First, you can follow the PCT north. Cross the north-south jeep trail, then go southwest down into a small creek bed. Just after you cross the creek bed, the PCT turns northwest. As you cross the creek bed, turn on your timer or start pace-counting. Keep trekking NW for 11-13 minutes, or about 950 yards. At this point, you may be able to hear the traffic and see the sign posts along Highway S1. There is a small but distinct trail that leads up the side of a bank about 100 yards to Highway S1 and the Lucky 5 gate.

Second, from the junction of the PCT and the two jeep trails, follow the N→S jeep trail south. Almost immediately, you cross a small creek bed, then turn northwest. Continue northwest along this jeep trail 0.7 mile to a gate and Highway S1. The Lucky 5 Ranch gate is across the road.

Given that Stephenson Peak road crosses the PCT, we recommend that you begin this hike from the Lucky 5 Ranch gate and go N→S. It is better to solve navigational problems at the beginning of the day, when you are fresh, than to encounter them at the end of the day, when you may be tired.

🚐 **Lucky 5 Ranch Gate on Highway S1**. From Stephenson Peak road, go N 9.7 miles on Highway S1 to the gated entrance to the Lucky 5 Ranch at Deer Park road. Park on the west side of the road near the Lucky 5 Gate. The PCT does not touch this point. There are two ways to reach it.

First, immediately across Highway S1 to the east is a gate. Just before you reach it, a small but distinct trail curls down to the left. Follow it less than 100 yards to the PCT, which, although not marked at this point, is obvious. Take a left to go north toward San Felipe Valley, a right to go south toward Pioneer Mail and Stephenson Peak road.

Second, when you reach the gate, cross it and follow the jeep trail 0.7 mile southeast to a creek bed. Here the jeep trail turns north. In less than 0.1 mile north, you intersect an east-bound jeep trail and the PCT.

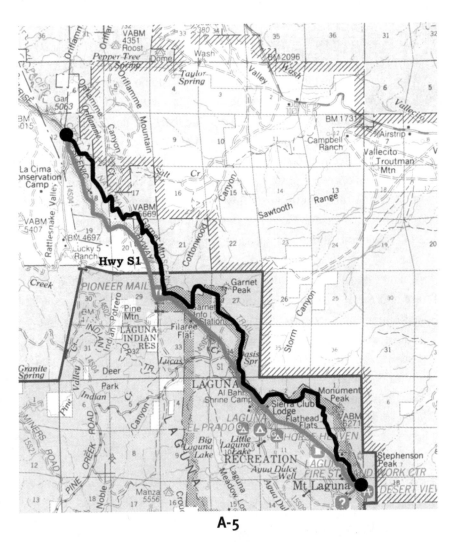

A-5

Lodging tip in the Laguna area: The Mt. Laguna Lodge (619) 484-1070, less than a mile south of the Desert View Overlook, features rustic cabins at reasonable prices. The lodge has a general store, and there is a restaurant across Highway S1.

Hike 6—Lucky 5 Ranch Gate on Highway S1 to Highway 78

PCT: 19.7 miles
Hike: 19.7 miles
Map: A-6 (Cleveland NF)
Difficulty: Moderate
Direction: S→N (Access/Elevation)

MOUNTAIN WEATHER

When we woke on the March morning we were to do this hike, we were greeted with pouring rain and wind howling from the northwest at over 30 miles an hour. We want to point out that there are dangers associated with long hikes through remote areas. Our goal was to do as much of the PCT as we could, one day at a time, with a keen eye toward safety.

The rain abated and we began, but it was still cold and windy. We started the hike with three layers—long-sleeve capilene shirt, Patagonia jacket, and Gore-Tex shell, together with gloves and a wool hat. This combination did not vary for the first ninety minutes of the hike.

Once the sun came out, we realized that we had made a navigational error. It cost us only a few minutes, but it could have been serious had we not recognized the error before we had descended another thousand feet. With the sun warming things, we began to shed layers; however, our hands were still so cold that it took a few minutes to undo our boots to rearrange socks, another reminder that the elements can test both endurance and decision-making capabilities.

Hike. (Originally, we wanted to start this hike by following an abandoned jeep trail that heads NE away from Cuyamaca Reservoir to the PCT (4770). This makes the hike shorter, but the recent increase in the number of NO TRESPASSING—YOU WILL BE PROSECUTED signs argues against this route choice. We strongly discourage anyone from violating the property rights of others, particularly when the property owner posts NO TRESPASSING signs.)

From the Lucky 5 Ranch gate, use either of the options described in Hike 5 to find the PCT. Then, go N 3.2 miles to a faint, abandoned jeep trail that leads southwest to Cuyamaca Reservoir. Continues N 2.4 miles to a road junction (3860) in Chariot Canyon. In another 4.9 miles you intersect Rodriguez Spur Truck Trail (3650). From here, you skirt around Granite Mountain and follow a ridge line 5.1 miles before descending into Earthquake Valley. In 2.9 miles, you intersect Highway S2 (2275), which you parallel for 0.8 mile, cross, and then go 0.4 mile to a crossing of Highway 78 (2252) in San Felipe Valley.

see map A-7A

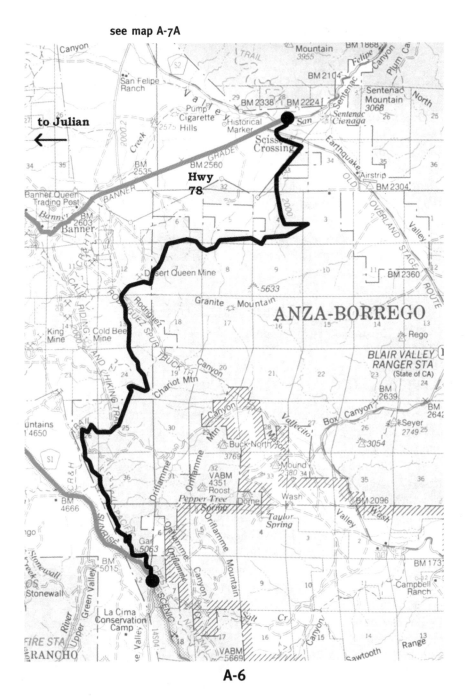

A-6

🚗 **Highway 78.** From the Lucky 5 Ranch gate, go N 4.2 miles on Highway S1 to Highway 79 (not shown on map A-6). Turn right (NW) and go 5.8 miles to Highway 78 just east of Julian (not shown on Map A-6).

Turn right (SE) on Highway 78 and go 11.4 miles toward Borrego Springs to Highway S2. Go south a little over 0.1 mile on S2 to where the PCT crosses the road. The PCT also crosses Highway 78 a little over 0.1 mile east of the junction of Highways 78/S2. There are several parking options in the area.

Dining tip in the Julian area. Julian is a pleasant mountain town. It is not far from San Diego, so it tends to be popular, especially on weekends, even in the dead of winter. There are several restaurants in the area, but one stands out as exceptional: Tom's Chicken Shack. It is located 3.9 miles west of the intersection of Highways 78/79 in Julian. It serves "family dinners," an outstanding value at $9.95, that include juice, soup or salad, buttermilk biscuits, choice of potatoes, entree (fried, broiled, or oven-baked chicken, chicken livers, grilled ham, or charbroiled ground beef 'n mushrooms—prime rib on the weekends—and dessert). Value is a great concept, but the food here is also exceptionally good!

Hike 7—Highway 78 to Barrel Spring TH

PCT: 23.9 miles
Hike: 23.9 miles
Maps: A-7A and A-7B (Cleveland NF)
Difficulty: Difficult

Hike. This hike is longer than we like for a single day, especially during the summer, when temperatures can easily reach triple digits every day. If this were an unbelievably stunning hike, we would try to break it into two pieces. In fact, there is one access point east of the PCT from Grapevine Canyon road. However, this road requires both a high-clearance 4WD and a good map, not to mention good navigational skills. We think that for some, this 23.9-mile segment is a doable day hike. The hike itself is mostly shadeless as you undulate up and down through the hills and valleys that parallel Highway S2 and San Felipe Valley to the west and Hoover Canyon to the east before arriving at the Barrel Spring TH (3445). Hiking in a few miles at either end will give you an idea of what the entire hike is like.

Barrel Spring TH. From the junction of Highway S2 and Highway 78 in San Felipe Valley, go N 12.2 miles on Highway S2 to Highway S22. Turn right (E) on Highway S22 and go 1.0 mile to a parking area where the PCT crosses the highway.

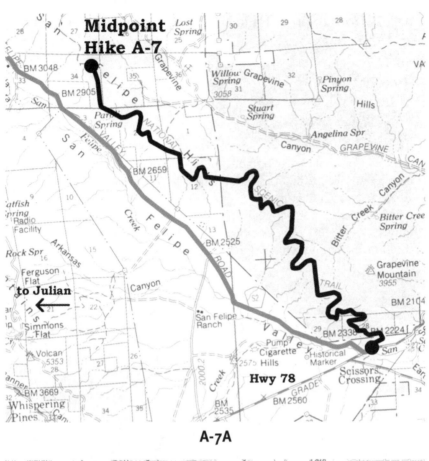

A-7A

A-7B

Hike 8—Barrel Spring TH to Highway 79 southwest of Warner Springs

PCT: 8.6 miles
Hike: 8.6 miles
Map: A-8 (Cleveland NF)
Difficulty: Easy

Hike. Today was Pat's turn to hike. We both hiked 2.1 miles from the Barrel Spring TH (3445) over a broad ridge and into an open valley where a faint jeep trail crosses the PCT (3285). I returned to the car. Pat continued N 1.7 miles to San Ysidro Creek (3355), then 2.8 miles to a ridgetop jeep road (3510), where I met her. We hiked 2.0 miles further to Highway 79 (3040). We spent a good deal of time chasing cows off the trail. Pat was happy to have done the whole segment herself. She said it

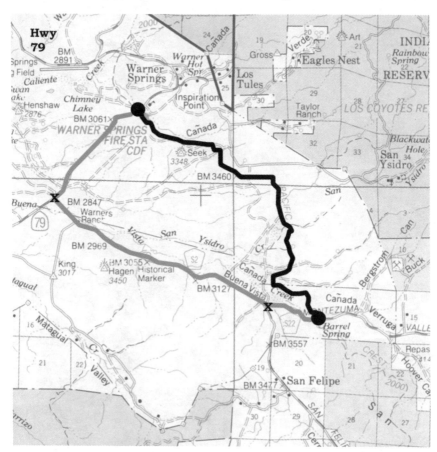

A-8

helped build her confidence and allowed her to hone her map and compass skills. (We strongly recommend that you carry a compass and map wherever and whenever you hike. In this area, there are several crossing trails that lead in different directions. Furthermore, when the sun disappears behind clouds, or fog or rain storm appears, it is very easy to become disoriented.)

Highway 79 southwest of Warner Springs. From the Barrel Spring TH, retrace your route W 1.0 mile on Highway S22 to Highway S2. Turn right (NW) and go 4.7 miles to Highway 79. Turn right (NE) and go 2.4 miles to Canada Verde Creek, where the PCT crosses Highway 79. There are a fire station, Warner Union School, and a small parking area just north of the creek.

Pat and PCT sign on Highway S22 near Barrel Spring

Warner Springs to San Gorgonio Pass

Overview

PCT: 101.4 miles
Day Hikes (8): 110.8 miles
Declination: 13° E

The PCT proceeds from Warner Springs (3040) through Chihuahua and Terwilliger valleys before ascending into the San Jacinto Mountains (8000+ feet). It then follows spectacular Fuller Ridge before descending 7000 feet to San Gorgonio Pass (1360) west of Palm Springs.

Hike 1—Highway 79 southwest of Warner Springs to Indian Flats CG Road 9S05

PCT: 8.8 miles
Hike: 9.2 miles
Map: B-1 (Cleveland NF)
Difficulty: Easy
Direction: N→S (Access)

🥾 **Hike.** From Canada Verde Creek (3040), where the PCT crosses Highway 79, you walk 1.8 miles around the Warner Springs golf course. You cross Highway 79 (2930) west of Warner Springs before beginning the 4.9-mile climb NE up Agua Caliente Creek to a side canyon (3520). Upon leaving the canyon and creek, you hike NW 2.1 miles to Lost Valley road (4170). From this clearly marked junction with the PCT, Lost Valley road descends S 0.4 mile (730-770 yards) to paved Indian Flats CG Road 9S05.

🚗 **Highway 79 southwest of Warner Springs.** From the Barrel Spring TH, where you started the last hike in Section A, retrace your route W 1.0 mile on Highway S22 to Highway S2. Turn right (NW) and go 4.7 miles to Highway 79. Turn right (NE) and go 2.4 miles to Canada

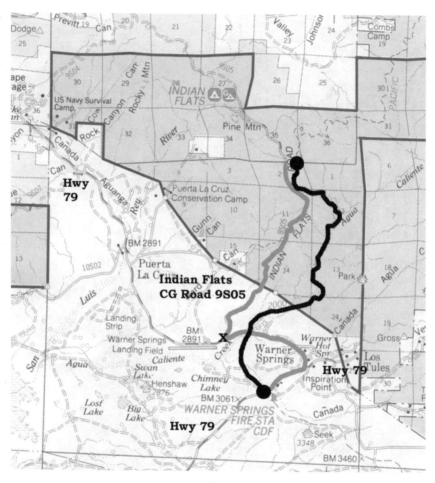

B-1

Verde Creek, where the PCT crosses Highway 79. There are a fire station, Warner Union School, and a small parking area just north of the creek.

🚐 **Indian Flats CG Road 9S05.** From Canada Verde Creek southwest of Warner Springs, go N 2.8 miles on Highway 79 to Indian Flats CG Road 9S05. Turn right (NE) on one-lane, paved 9S05—follow the INDIAN FLATS CG sign—and go 4.6 miles to a gate on the east side of the road near a sign that reads NO CAMPFIRES. Hike past the gate, up Lost Valley road 0.4 mile (730-770 yards) to the PCT (4170), which is well-marked. Turn left to go north to Chihuahua Valley, right to go south to Warner Springs.

BOY SCOUTS LOST

We suggest you do this hike N→S. Although we do not consider it difficult to find Lost Valley road, if you do miss it, you may get confused.
Warner Springs Ranch and Highway 79, on the other hand, are hard to
miss. We watched a large contingent of Boy Scouts try to find the PCT
from Indian Flats CG Road 9S05 and were amazed that even the Scout
Master had to stop us twice to ask if "it" (the PCT) was "up there." We
would rather you have trouble finding it at the beginning of the hike
than at the end of the hike.

Hike 2—Indian Flats CG Road 9S05 to Chihuahua Valley Road

PCT: 8.9 miles
Hike: 9.3 miles
Map: B-2 (Cleveland NF)
Difficulty: Easy

Hike. From Indian Flats CG Road 9S05, go N 0.4 mile (730-770
yards on Lost Valley road) to the PCT (4170). Go N 1.1 miles on the PCT—
a continuation of Lost Valley road at this point—to a side road (4450) that
leads to Lost Valley Spring. Continue E 3.2 miles on the PCT across three
small ridge systems before turning north for the final 4.6 miles to
Chihuahua Valley road (5050).

Chihuahua Valley Road—preferred option. Retrace your route
on Indian Flats CG Road 9S05 to Highway 79. Turn right (N) on Highway
79 and go 8.8 miles to paved Chihuahua Valley road (this intersection is
not shown on Map B-2). Turn right (E) on Chihuahua Valley road and go
6.4 miles to a sharp turn in the road and a sign that reads BSA CAMP LVSR.
At this junction, Chihuahua Valley road veers to the right (S), but you go
straight (E). Almost immediately, there is a private dirt road that bears to
the left (NE) and a dirt road that bears to the right (E). You bear to the
right (E)—follow the signs for the Lost Valley Scout Reservation—and go
4.8 miles to a ridge and the PCT. You'll pass the Sky Oaks Biological
Station along the way.

Chihuahua Valley Road—second option (4WD only). One-lane
paved Lost Valley Road 9S05 continues N 1.7 miles to a gated entrance to
the Indian Flats CG. Less than 100 yards before the gate, unmarked and
unpaved FR 9S05 jogs to the right. This, rough, dirt, 4WD road eventually intersects Chihuahua Valley road 2.0 miles west of the BSA CAMP LVSR

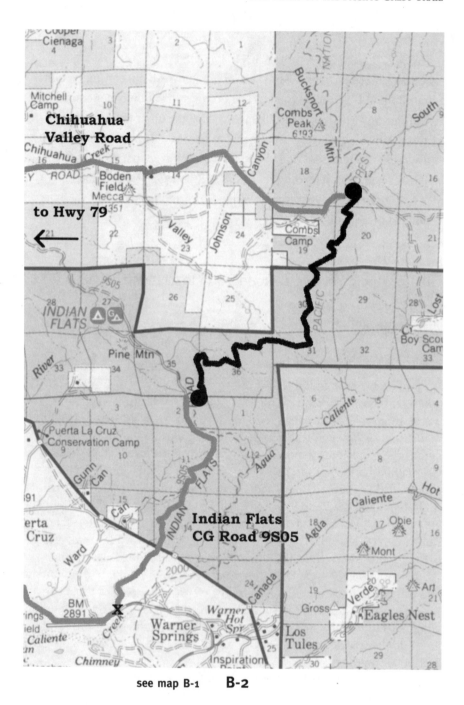

see map B-1   **B-2**

sign. If you have 4WD, this is an option. For the rest of us, the safest route choice is the "preferred option" above.

Hike 3—Chihuahua Valley Road to Tule Canyon Truck Trail

PCT: 10.0 miles
Hike: 10.3 miles
Map: B-3 (Cleveland NF)
Difficulty: Easy

🚶 **Hike.** The PCT heads north as it slowly climbs 1.9 miles along the east slope of Bucksnort Mountain to the east shoulder of Combs Peak (5595). Continue N 2.4 miles to the head of Tule Canyon (4710). It is another 5.7 miles to Tule Canyon Truck Trail (3640). Follow this trail W

see map B-4

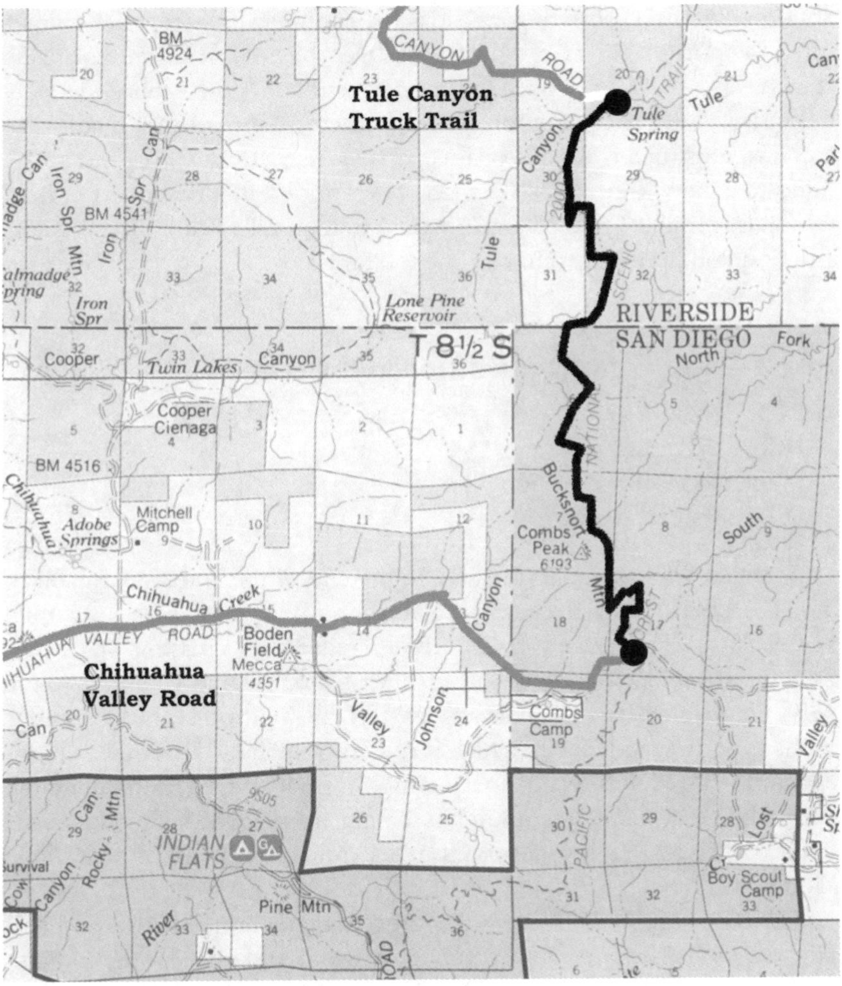

B-3

0.3 mile (530-570 yards) to the State Park boundary fence. There is a small parking area just before the fence that defines the boundary. (The State Park boundary is not shown on the USFS or PCT guide maps, but there is definitely a fence at the boundary when you get there.)

Kirby Road to Tule Canyon Truck Trail. (Also refer to Map B-4 for a more complete picture of the roads that lead to Tule Canyon.) Retrace your route along Chihuahua Valley road to Highway 79. Turn right (N) and go 9.3 miles to Highway 371. Turn right (N) and go 16.4 miles to Kirby road. (If you are coming from the junction of Highways 74/371 to the north, go S 4.3 miles on Highway 371 to Kirby road.)

When you reach Kirby road, follow the sign for Terwilliger. First go S 1.0 mile. This paved road turns east for 1.0 mile, then turns S again. You are now on paved Terwilliger road. Go S 3.8 miles to where Terwilliger turns to the right (W). Go right a little over 0.1 mile to a sign that reads TULE CYN. SOUTH. Turn left (S) on this dirt road and go 1.3 miles to a partially destroyed street sign on the east side of the road that reads TULE CANYON. This road is the Tule Canyon Truck Trail. Turn left (E) and go 2.2 miles to a gate at the Anza-Borrego State Park boundary fence. On foot, follow this trail 0.3 mile (530-570 yards) to the PCT (3640). (If you get to Tule Canyon Spring, you have gone too far.)

Hike 4—Tule Canyon Truck Trail to Highway 74

PCT: 15.4 miles
Hike: 15.7 miles
Map: B-4 (San Bernardino NF)
Difficulty: Moderate

Hike. From the parking area at the end of the Tule Canyon Truck Trail near the Anza-Borrego State Park boundary fence, hike E 0.3 mile (530-570) yards to the PCT. Go NE 2.9 miles to a crossing of Coyote Canyon road (3500). Continue N 3.6 miles, skirting Table Mountain to the west, before crossing yet another jeep trail (4075). Proceed NW 3.9 miles to the next dirt road (4910), which is not far from Table Mountain's highest point. The PCT descends to Alkali Wash (4540), then climbs along the west slope of Lookout Mountain before it intersects Pine-to-Palms Highway 74 (4919), a total of 5.0 miles from the dirt road near Table Mountain.

Highway 74. Retrace your route to the junction of Kirby road and Highway 371. Turn right (NE) on Highway 371 and go 4.3 miles to Pine-to-Palms Highway 74. Turn right (E) on Highway 74 and go 1.0 mile to the PCT (4919) and a TH parking area on the north side of the road.

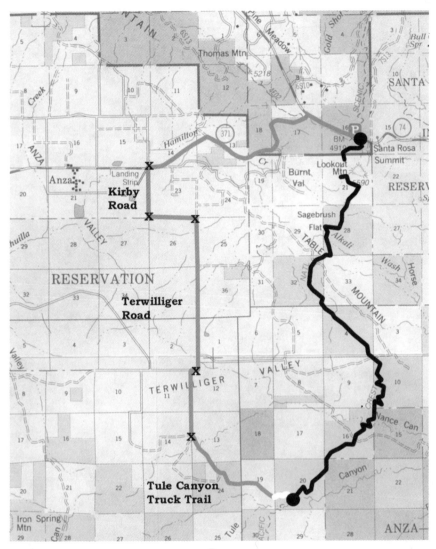

B-4

Hike 5—Highway 74 to Fobes TH

PCT: 14.2 miles
Hike: 15.7 miles
Map: B-5 (San Bernardino NF)
Difficulty: Moderate

Hike. From the TH on Highway 74, hike N 3.7 miles to Penrod Canyon (5040). In another 2.0 miles, you reach Road 6S01A (5700). In the next 6.0 miles, you pass Lion Peak, Pyramid Peak, and Little Desert Peak

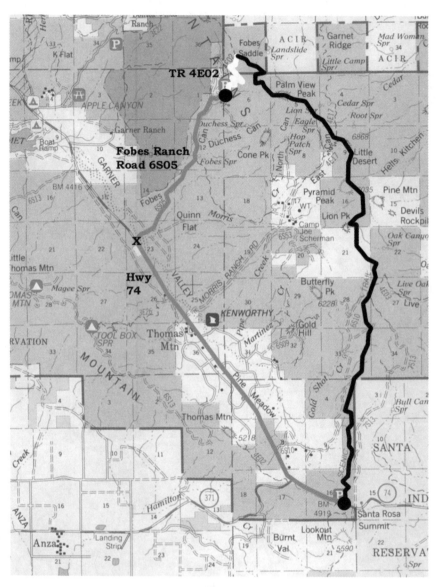

B-5

before arriving at Cedar Spring Trail 4E17, which descends southwest to Morris Ranch. Continue NW 3.5 miles past Palm View Peak to Fobes Saddle (5990), then hike 1.5 miles down Fobes Trail 4E02 to its TH.

🚐 **Fobes TH**. Return to the junction of Highway 371 and Highway 74. Turn right (NW) on Highway 74 and go 5.7 miles to Fobes Ranch Road 6S05. Turn right (NE) and go 3.9 miles to the Fobes Trail 4E02 TH. You'll need a wilderness permit, available from the Ranger Station in Idyllwild,

25925 Village Center Drive. (Some of the signs along the road refer to Trail 4E02 as Trail 4E04. As far as we can tell, the correct reference should be Trail 4E02. No matter, you should have no problem finding the TH.)

Hike 6—Fobes TH to Devils Slide TH

PCT: 12.3 miles
Hike: 16.3 miles
Map: B-6 (San Bernardino NF)
Difficulty: Moderate

THE HAIL STORM AT SADDLE JUNCTION

A few years before we began this project, we hiked in this area with friends Mel and Carrie from San Diego. We met in Palm Springs for the weekend and had decided to take the tram from the 115° desert floor— it was mid-August—to the ridge above. We would hike to Devils Saddle by one route, and take another route back to the tram for the trip down. In all, it would be a 12-mile hike. I looked at it as a way to break in my brand new, pink orienteering shoes—shoes so grotesque that Carrie would pretend not to be with us when we met other hikers on the trail.

As we approached Saddle Junction, the cumulus clouds that had been mounting all morning turned black, and as we stood under some trees at the junction, they began to unload. Rain turned to hail, calm turned to wind, and temperatures fell as the storm unleashed its fury. We moved to the shelter of some nearby rocks, but could not escape the hail, some two inches of it in less than 10 minutes. It pounded our nylon jackets without mercy, leaving behind pock marks on our arms and torso. All of us were dressed only in shorts, T-shirt, and nylon wind breaker. That was it. As the water and hail stones swirled beneath our feet and we began to shiver, we all knew that we were in one boat-load of trouble and that our only option was to start down the west side of the mountain to warmer air below and the town of Idyllwild. During that 2.5-mile trek to warmth, we also swore that we would never again go to the mountains without a day pack filled with emergency gear, a promise we have kept ever since.

see map B-7

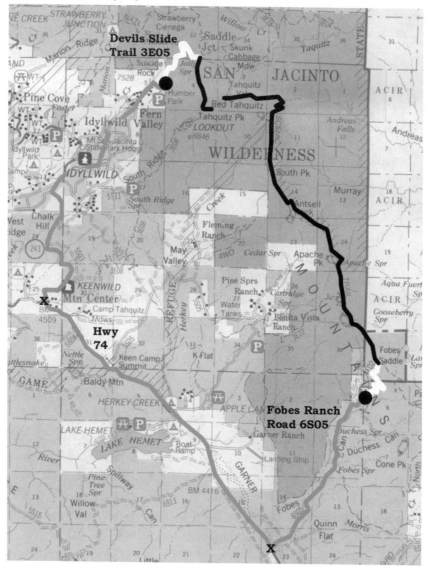

B-6

🥾 **Hike.** From the Fobes Trail 4E02 TH, hike 1.5 miles up Trail 4E02 to the PCT (5990). The PCT goes up 2.6 miles to the Apache Spring trail (7430). Continue NW 6.3 miles past Apache Peak and Southwell Peak. Here, you reach the top of the ascent (8380) above Andreas Canyon's deep gorge. The trail turns W and in 2.1 miles intersects Tahquitz Peak Trail 3E08 (8570). Today's PCT hike ends 1.3 miles further at Saddle

Junction (8100). From here, hike 2.5 miles down Devils Slide Trail 3E05 to Fern Valley Road 5S22, which leads to the mountain town of Idyllwild, where you will find tourists, shops, tourists, restaurants, tourists, grocery stores, tourists, the Idyllwild Ranger Station, 25925 Village Center Drive, and more tourists.

🚗 **Devils Slide TH**. Return to the junction of Fobes Ranch road and Highway 74. Turn right (N) on Highway 74 and go 6.9 miles to Highway 243. Turn right (N) and go 4.4 miles to the center of Idyllwild. Turn right—follow the signs to Fern Valley road—and go 0.7 mile to South Circle Drive. Turn right and follow the signs to Fern Valley road and Humber Park, the parking area for this popular TH. (You will need a US Forest Service permit to hike up Devils Slide Trail 3E05. Permits are available from the Idyllwild Ranger Station, 25925 Village Center Drive on a first-come, first-serve basis.)

Hike 7—Devils Slide TH to Fuller Ridge TH

PCT: 12.0 miles
Hike: 14.5 miles
Map: B-7 (San Bernardino NF)
Difficulty: Moderate
Direction: N→S (Risk)

🥾 **Hike**. Because snow can linger along steep Fuller Ridge into early July, we recommend you do this hike N→S. It is far wiser to discover that the trail is too dangerous for you at the beginning of the hike than to have to turn around after you have hiked over 10 miles.

From the Devils Slide 3E05 TH at the end of Fern Valley road, hike 2.5 miles up Trail 3E05 to Saddle Junction (8100) and the PCT. Turn left and go N 1.8 miles to the Wellmans Cienaga trail (9030), then W 2.3 miles to Marion Ridge Trail 3E17 (8070). Continue 2.1 miles to a crossing of the North Fork San Jacinto River (8830). In another 1.9 miles you reach impressive Fuller Ridge (8725), which you follow 3.9 miles to the Fuller Ridge TH (7750).

🚗 **Fuller Ridge TH**. Return to the junction of Fern Valley road and Highway 243 in Idyllwild. Turn right (N) on Highway 243 and go 8.1 miles to Black Mountain Road 4S01. Turn right (E) on this dirt road and go 1.7 miles to a major gate, which is closed in winter. Continue 3.1 miles to the Black Mountain Lookout cutoff, and another 1.1 miles to the Black Mountain Group CG. Staying on the same road, you intersect the PCT in another 1.1 miles. The Fuller Ridge TH parking area is 0.2 mile further along FR 4S01.

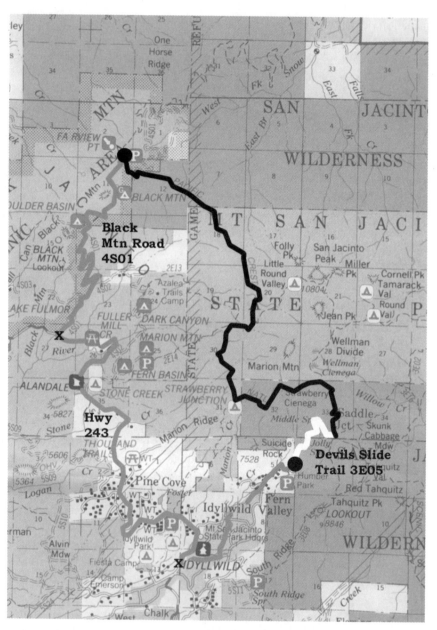

B-7

Hike 8—Fuller Ridge TH to I-10 in San Gorgonio Pass

PCT: 19.8 miles
Hike: 19.8 miles
Map: B-8 (San Bernardino NF)
Difficulty: Moderate
Direction: S→N (Elevation)

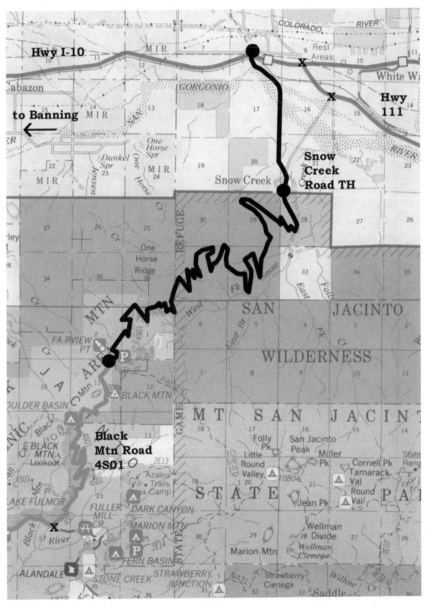

B-8

Hike. From the Fuller Ridge TH, hike NW 0.2 mile to Black Mountain Road 4S01 (7670). From here, the PCT zigs and zags down the northwest slope of the San Jacinto Mountains into the San Gorgonio River Basin. You cross the West Fork of Snow Creek (3200) 11.8 miles from Road 4S01. In another 4.2 miles you intersect paved Snow Canyon road (1725). In another 1.0 mile you intersect Falls Creek road, which you follow 0.2 mile to Snow Creek road (1230). If you end the hike here, you shorten it by 2.4 miles. The full 19.6-mile hike ends in the town of West Palm Springs, where you go under I-10 to Tamarack road.

Snow Creek Road. Return to the junction of Black Mountain Road 4S01 and Highway 243. Turn right (N) on Highway 243 and go 16.9 miles on this steep, winding road, to the town of Banning and Highway I-10. (These two roads are not shown on the USFS map provided here.) Go E 12.3 miles on I-10 to Highway 111. Bear right (SE) and go 1.0 mile on Highway 111 to Snow Creek road. Turn right (SW) and go 1.6 miles to Fall Creek road and the PCT. Follow Fall Creek road—also the PCT at this point—SE 0.2 mile to unmarked Snow Canyon road. Go east less than 100 yards, to where vehicle progress is stopped by a gate. At this point, Snow Canyon road and the PCT are one and the same.

Tamarack Road north of the I-10 underpass. From the entrance to Highway I-10 in Banning, go E 11.7 miles to the Verbena Avenue exit. Go N less than 0.1 mile, then take a left (W) on Tamarack road. Go W 0.3 mile on Tamarack road to where the PCT crosses it. The PCT crosses under I-10 a few hundred yards to the south.

San Gorgonio Pass to Interstate 15 near Cajon Pass

Overview

PCT: 132.7 miles
Day Hikes (9): 133.1 miles
Declination: 13° E

B eginning in the Colorado Desert at San Gorgonio Pass (1360), the PCT crosses the San Andreas Fault, then climbs to the top of and runs the entire length of the San Bernardino Mountains crest. It passes Onyx Summit (8510) and popular Big Bear Lake as it makes its way west to Little Bear Springs Trail Camp (6600), Holcomb Creek, and Deep Creek Bridge (4580) near Lake Arrowhead. It then turns north past Deep Creek Hot Springs (3535) on its way to Mojave River Forks Reservoir Dam (3131) and around Silverwood Lake (3390). It ends at I-15 near Cajon Pass (3000).

DAY HIKE LOGISTICS

In this section, we encountered our first major logistical problem. The first hike, 29.5 miles, is longer than we would recommend for most day-hikers. Unfortunately, two access points that would enable us to break this hike into two pieces are "off limits." Both of these, the Whitewater Trout Farm and the East Fork of Mission Creek, are on private property, and the owners are unwilling to allow access to the PCT.

The problem is simple: users have trashed both areas. The result is that the land owners have said, "no more access." Please respect their wishes and stay off their property.

Hike 1—San Gorgonio Pass to Mission Creek Trail Camp

PCT: 29.5 miles
Hike: 29.5 miles
Maps: C-1A and C-1B (San Bernardino NF)
Difficulty: Difficult
Direction: N→S (Elevation)

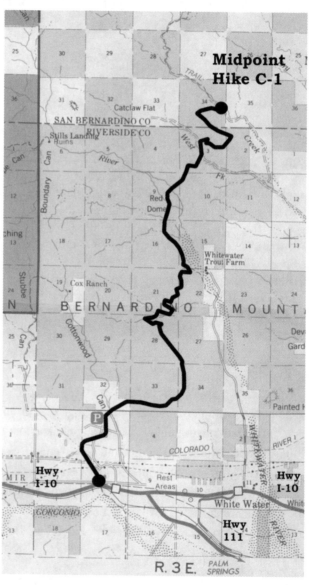

C-1A

Hike. We recommend you do this hike N→S. There is a significant elevation change of over 6000 feet, from 1360 at San Gorgonio Pass to 7965 at Mission Creek Trail Camp. We also suggest that you end it at the Cottonwood TH (1850), which reduces the hike to only 27.4 miles. We do not rate this hike very highly because it travels through harsh terrain with little relief from the sun. There is a federal wilderness area to the west of the PCT, but because there are too many hikers who use it, the PCT is forced to follow a less desirable route in this region.

Hiking 2.1 miles on the PCT, you first skirt West Palm Springs Village to the west, then turn NE to the Cottonwood TH (1850). The trail turns east for 1.5 miles through Gold Canyon, then turns north and parallels the Whitewater River Canyon for 5.5 miles to the canyon's mouth (2285). Next, in 3.5 miles, you cross the West Fork of Mission Creek (2918), then the East Fork (3060) 3.3 miles further. The trail continues north, paralleling Mission Creek, 6.4 miles to Forks Springs (4830). This is a difficult stretch of trail because of frequent washouts and rugged creek crossings. The PCT bends to the northwest, then west, still paralleling Mission Creek as it gradually climbs for the final 7.2 miles to Mission Creek Trail Camp (7965). (As the best part of this hike is the last 7.2 miles, you might consider doing this as a 14.4-mile round trip, beginning at Mission Creek Trail Camp.)

Tamarack Road north of the I-10 underpass. From the Highway I-10 exit in Banning (not shown on Map C-1), go E 11.7 miles on Highway I-10 to the Verbena Avenue exit. Go north less than 0.1 mile, then take a left (W) on Tamarack road. Go W 0.3 mile on Tamarack road to where the PCT crosses it. The PCT crosses under I-10 a few hundred yards to the south.

Cottonwood TH. From the junction of Tamarack road and the PCT, go E 0.1 mile to Cottonwood road. Turn left (N) on paved Cottonwood road and go 1.2 miles to a rough dirt road that leads another 0.5 mile to the Cottonwood TH parking area. A sign here states: CANADA 2384, MEXICO 217. (The sign numbers are close. You are 214.1 miles north of the Mexican border and 2452.6 miles south of the Canadian border.)

Mission Creek Trail Camp. From the Verbena exit, go W on I-10 to the Highway 38 (6th Avenue/Downtown) exit in Redlands. Go E 33.0 miles on Highway 38 to the Heart Bar CG (Coon Creek/Fish Creek) turnoff. Turn right (SE) and go 1.2 miles to 1N05. Turn right (W) on 1N05 and go 5.2 miles to a ridge where the PCT crosses the road. Go down 0.2 mile on 1N05 to 1N93. Bear to the right 0.4 mile—do not take 1N37 to the left—to the Mission Creek Trail Camp. (The San Bernardino NF map refers to the Mission Creek TC as the Mission Springs TC. They are one and the same place.)

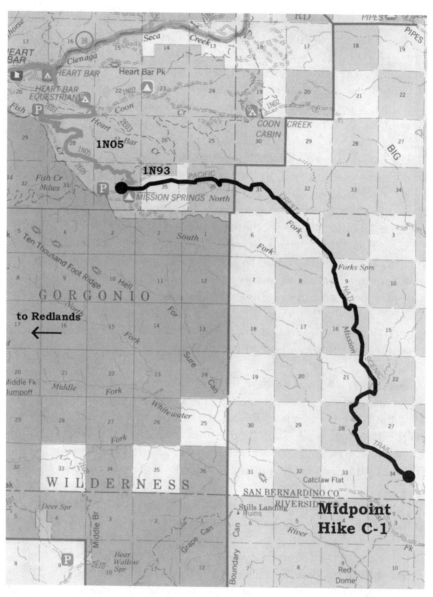

C-1B

(Most even-numbered roads (e.g., I-70, US 2, WA 20) run east-west. Most odd-numbered roads (e.g., I-5, US 97, CA 99) run north-south. Some roads do not follow these conventions. For example, Highway 38 goes east from Redlands to Onyx Summit, then north for a short distance before turning west to end at the west end of Big Bear Lake. We try to follow the north, east, south, west road-naming conventions when describing directions. However, when we encounter an exception to the rule, such as Highway 38, we use the directions that follow the orientation on the map.)

George on the PCT near Vincent Gap

Hike 2—Mission Creek Trail Camp to the dirt road east of Onyx Summit

PCT: 12.3 miles
Hike: 12.3 miles
Map: C-2 (San Bernardino NF)
Difficulty: Moderate

🚶 **Hike.** The PCT leads N 0.6 mile, to where it crosses 1N05 (8240), the road on the ridge you crossed on your way down to Mission Creek Trail Camp. You cross the same road again (8115) in another 0.8 mile. The trail continues 5.2 miles to Coon Creek Road 1N02 (8090). You cross several trails and jeep roads in the next 5.7 miles on your way to the dirt road (8510) east of Onyx Summit.

🚗 **The dirt road east of Onyx Summit.** From the Mission Creek Trail Camp, retrace your route to Highway 38. Turn right (E) on Highway 38 and go 5.8 miles to the Onyx Summit parking area. From the parking area, hike E 50 yards to a fence. (A N-S jeep road, 1N01, traverses this area.) Continue E 100 yards past the fence to the PCT.

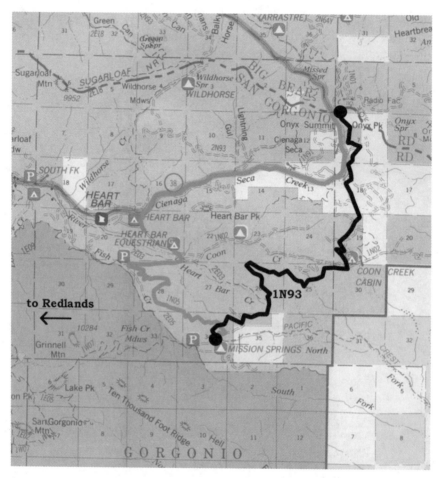

C-2

Hike 3—The dirt road east of Onyx Summit to Highway 18

PCT: 13.6 miles
Hike: 13.6 miles
Map: C-3 (San Bernardino NF)
Difficulty: Moderate

Hike. This is an enjoyable hike, much of it paralleling Highway 38. Again, you encounter several roads along the way. From the dirt road east of Onyx Summit, you go 3.2 miles to Broom Flat Road 2N01 (7885), then 2.4 miles to Road 2N04 (7155). In another 3.8 miles, you reach Arrastre Creek Road 2N02 (6775). Then, you descend 4.2 miles to Highway 18 (6829) north of Baldwin Lake.

🚐 **Highway 18**. From the dirt road east of Onyx Summit, go NW 10.2 miles on Highway 38 to the junction of Highways 18/38 in Big Bear City. Turn right (N) on Highway 18/38 and go 0.6 mile to where the roads separate. Turn right (NE) on Highway 18 and go 4.4 miles to Milepost 59 and the crest where the PCT crosses the road.

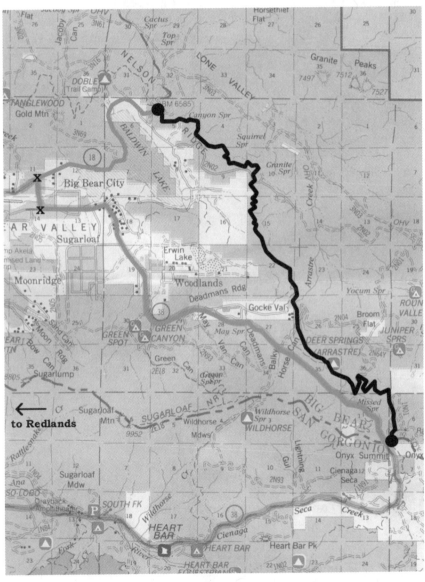

C-3

Hike 4—Highway 18 to Van Dusen Canyon Road 3N09

PCT: 8.9 miles
Hike: 8.9 miles
Map: C-4 (San Bernardino NF)
Difficulty: Easy

Hike. This is a pleasant, fairly level hike through the forests north of Big Bear Lake. It is the kind of hike you take friends on to show them a peaceful part of the PCT. From Highway 18 (6829), the PCT goes NW 2.0 miles to Doble Road 3N08 (6855), then turns SW for a 5.1-mile trek toward Gold Mountain, which you contour around on its north side, to a tributary of Caribou Creek (7560). In another 1.8 miles, you reach Van Dusen Canyon Road 3N09 (7260).

Van Dusen Canyon Road 3N09. Retrace your route 4.4 miles on Highway 18 to the junction of Highways 18/38 north of Big Bear City. Go straight (W) 0.5 mile on Highway 38 to Van Dusen Canyon Road 3N09. Turn right (N) on this partially paved road and go 2.8 miles to the PCT.

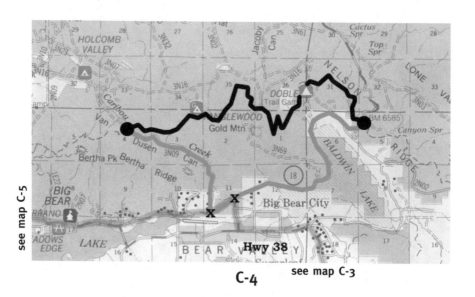

C-4   see map C-3

Hike 5—Van Dusen Canyon Road 3N09 to Little Bear Springs Trail Camp

PCT: 10.7 miles
Hike: 10.7 miles
Map: C-5 (San Bernardino NF)
Difficulty: Easy

ⓗ Hike. Another nice, fairly level hike through forest. After leaving Van Dusen Canyon Road 3N09 (7260), you cross two jeep trails before reaching Cougar Crest Trail 1E22 (7680) 2.7 miles into the hike. In another 0.8 mile, you cross Holcomb Valley Road 2N09 (7550). You cross Road 3N12 (7755) atop a saddle 2.8 miles further. The PCT descends from here 4.4 miles to Little Bear Springs Trail Camp (6600).

ⓡ Little Bear Springs Trail Camp. Retrace your route to Highway 38. Turn right (W) and go 5.9 miles to the town of Fawnskin. Turn right (NW) on briefly paved FR 3N14 Rim of the World Drive—follow the signs for Butler Peak, YMCA Camp Whittle, and the Hanna Flat and Big Pine CGs—and go 2.0 miles to YMCA Camp Whittle. Continue straight (N) on 3N14 and go 2.3 miles to the trail access to Little Bear Springs Trail Camp. There is a parking area where the PCT crosses both Holcomb Creek and Road 3N14. The trail camp is 0.2 mile east of this trail/creek/road crossing.

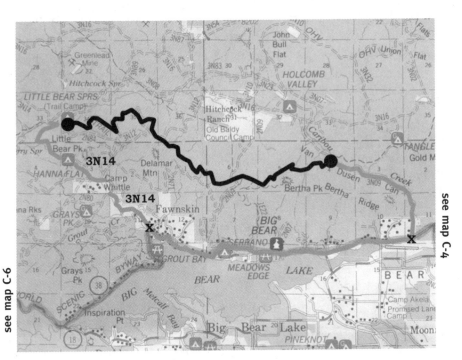

C-5

Hike 6—Little Bear Springs Trail Camp to Deep Creek Bridge

PCT: 12.8 miles
Hike: 13.0 miles
Map: C-6 (San Bernardino NF)
Difficulty: Moderate

Hike. Another great forest hike. Once across Holcomb Creek (6510), the PCT parallels it for some nine miles. At 6.8 miles into this hike, you intersect Crab Flats Road 3N16 and Road 3N93 (5465). In another 1.9 miles you reach the Holcomb Crossing Trail Camp (5190). From here, the PCT diverges from Holcomb Creek and continues W 4.1 miles to a 90-foot steel bridge over Deep Creek (4580).

A sign at the west side of the bridge says the PCT goes north from here. To reach the Splinter's TH, go south 100 yards to a small creek. Cross the creek to the east, then go south 50 yards to the TH parking area. From the bridge to the TH is 0.2 mile.

Deep Creek Bridge. Retrace your route to Highway 38. Turn right (W) and go 3.3 miles to Highway 18 (Highway 38 ends there.) Turn right (W) on spectacular Highway 18—amply named RIM OF THE WORLD SCENIC BYWAY—and go 12.3 miles to Running Springs and Highway 330. Bear right (NW), staying on Highway 18, and go 7.0 miles to Highway 173 and a sign for the town of Lake Arrowhead. (This is the only privately owned lake in the state of California.) Turn right (N) on Highway 173 and go 3.2 miles to Hook Creek road. Turn right (E) and go 2.3 miles to where the pavement ends. Go 1.0 mile on dirt 2N26Y to a large USFS map/sign that shows exactly how to get to the Splinter's TH. Bear left on 3N34 a little over 0.1 mile to 3N34C and a gate that is sometimes closed. Follow 3N34C 0.4 mile to the Splinter's TH parking area (not shown on the San Bernardino NF map).

Hike 7—Deep Creek Bridge to Highway 173 above Mojave River Forks Reservoir

PCT: 15.9 miles
Hike: 16.1 miles
Map: C-7 (San Bernardino NF)
Difficulty: Moderate
Direction: S→N (Elevation)

Hike. To reach the Deep Creek bridge from the Splinter's TH (0.2 mile), hike 50 yards north down to a small creek. Ford the creek and fol-see map C-5

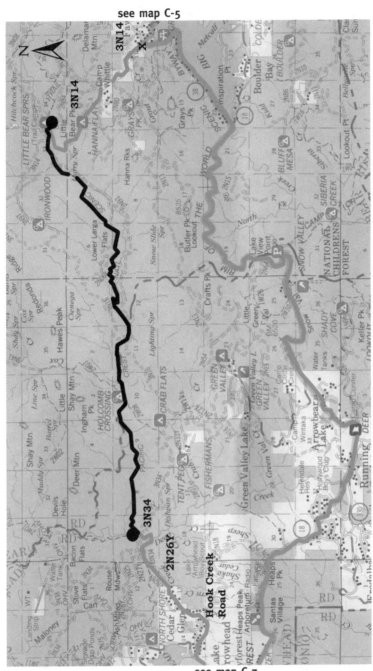

see map C-7

C-6

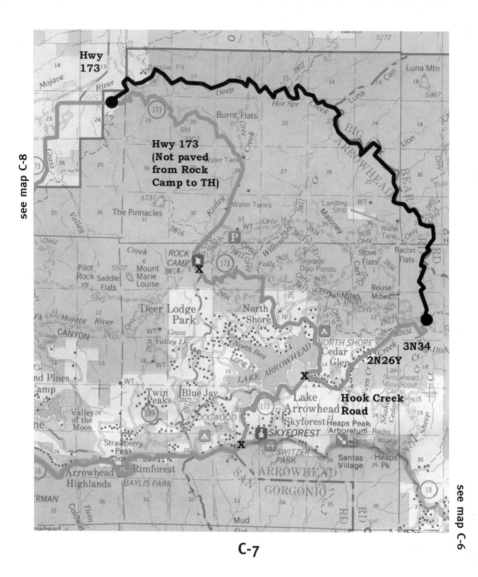

C-7

low the visible trail another 100 yards south to Deep Creek bridge. The PCT goes north from the west side of the bridge.

This hike follows Deep Creek north several miles, then turns west to Deep Creek Hot Spring. At 2.6 miles from the bridge (4580), you cross Bacon Flats Road 3N20 (4255). Deep Creek Hot Spring (3535) is 6.8 miles further along the trail. At 2.0 miles past the springs, another bridge (3315) crosses Deep Creek. In another 3.0 miles, you reach Mojave River Forks Reservoir dam (3131). It is another 1.5 miles to Highway 173 (3190).

🚗 **Highway 173 above Mojave River Forks Reservoir—most reliable option**. From the Splinter's TH, retrace your route to the intersection of Hook Creek road and Highway 173. Turn left (S) on Highway 173 and go 3.2 miles to Highway 18. Turn right (W) and go 6.7 miles to Highway 138. Turn right (N) and go 10.5 miles to the entrance to Silverwood Lake. (This intersection will be important at the end of the next hike, Hike 8.)

RESCUE ON HIGHWAY 173

I was on my way to field-check Highway 173. It was early April so I did not expect to meet many people. You can imagine my surprise when three miles from the summit, I spotted a family of four walking up the road. The father, a large man dressed in Army camouflage, waved at me and asked gruffly, "Do you have a cell phone?" I said, "Yes, but it probably won't work here." It didn't. When I asked what had happened, his 11-year-old son, also dressed in a camouflage suit, began to respond. His father ordered his son to "shut-up," and they began to walk up the hill. I asked them if they knew how far it was to the nearest town and he said, "less than a mile." I said, "it's over eight miles, let me give you a ride."

His wife stopped, grabbed her 13-year-old daughter by the arm, turned around, and walked back to my car. Her son also followed her example. The father reluctantly got in with his wife and kids. I asked the kids if they were thirsty, to which the father said, "No." I gave each of them a 32-ounce bottle of Gatorade, which was gone in less than 30 nanoseconds. When we reached the summit, the father opened the door to get out of the car. I asked him if he knew how far it was to Lake Arrowhead, to which he responded, "about a mile." I replied, "well, you can walk, but I am going to give your wife and kids a lift to town."

Having deposited the family at a filing station, my curiosity was piqued as to what had happened to their car. I returned to Highway 173 and discovered a 4WD Chevrolet Blazer in the middle of the road with one tire completely missing. I followed the tracks that the rim of the wheel had left 300 feet down the road to where the tire had come completely off the rim. Mystery solved, I proceeded toward Silverwood Lake, musing to myself how stupid some people are, and how unlucky that woman and her children were.

Continue straight (N)—stay on Highway 138—2.4 miles to Highway 173. Turn right (E) and go 7.7 miles to where the PCT crosses the highway.

🚗 **Highway 173 above Mojave River Forks Reservoir—a shorter, but more questionable option.** From the Splinter's TH, retrace your route to the intersection of Hook Creek road and Highway 173. Turn right (N) on Highway 173 and go 7.0 miles to where the pavement ends. Continue N 6.8 miles to the PCT. Sometimes, this unpaved segment of Highway 173 is gated closed. When it is open, this dirt road is a viable option.

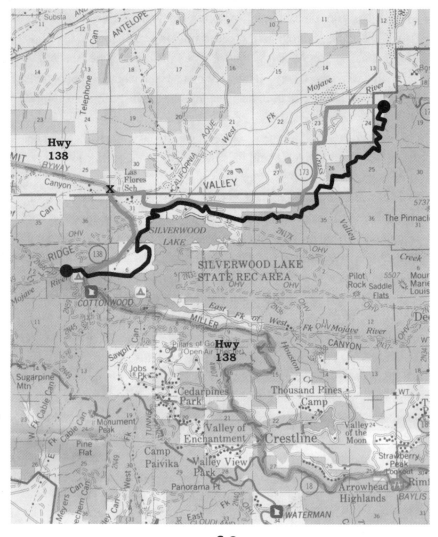

C-8

Hike 8—Highway 173 above Mojave River Forks Reservoir to Silverwood Lake Exit

PCT: 15.4 miles
Hike: 15.4 miles
Map: C-8 (San Bernardino NF)
Difficulty: Moderate

🚶 Hike. This hike follows Highway 173 as it winds to and around Silverwood Lake. At 3.9 miles into the hike, you cross Grass Valley Creek (3330). In another 5.5 miles, you cross FR 2N33 (3400) near the base of Cedar Springs Dam. The PCT follows roads for the next 1.2 miles, until it heads toward the lake shore. In another 4.8 miles you arrive at the entrance road to Silverwood Lake State Recreation Area (3390).

🚗 Silverwood Lake exit. Retrace your route W 7.7 miles on Highway 173 to Highway 138. Turn left (SW) and go 2.4 miles to the Cleghorn/Silverwood Lake exit. You can also start this hike at the exit, but parking there is limited. You best option is to follow paved Cleghorn road W 0.8 mile to a parking lot where the pavement ends. Walk back (east) along this road 0.2 mile to where the PCT touches the north side of the road.

Hike 9—Silverwood Lake Exit to I-15 near Cajon Pass

PCT: 13.6 miles
Hike: 13.6 miles
Map: C-9 (San Bernardino NF)
Difficulty: Moderate

🚶 Hike. This hike begins at the entrance road to Silverwood Lake, then turns NW. It parallels Highway 138 as it winds its way to Highway I-15 near Cajon Pass. Near the halfway point, 7.1 miles from Silverwood Lake and 6.5 miles from your destination, you cross a dry creek bed in Little Horsethief Canyon (3570). At 4.9 miles past the canyon, you cross Road 3N44 (3355), then descend to Highway I-15 near Cajon Pass (3000).

🚗 I-15 near Cajon Pass. From the Cleghorn/Silverwood Lake exit off Highway 138, go NE 2.4 miles on Highway 138 to Highway 173. Bear left (NW)—stay on Highway 138—and go 8.2 miles to the Cajon Junction exit off Highway I-15. When you reach the east frontage road, turn left (S) and go 0.5 mile to a parking area near the Santa Fe Trail Pioneers Memorial. The PCT goes west through the tunnel under Highway I-15 just south of the parking area.

see map C-8

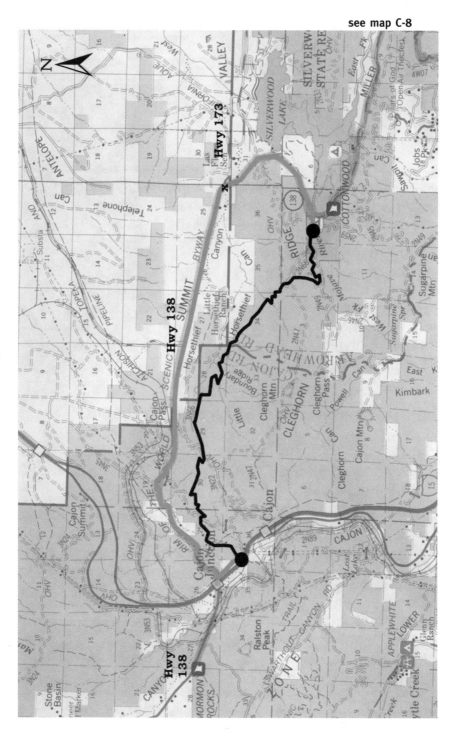

C-9

Interstate 15 near Cajon Pass
to Agua Dulce

Overview

PCT: 110.2 miles
Day Hikes (13): 110.2 miles
Declination: 13.5° E

The first 25 miles of Section D climb from I-15 near Cajon Pass (3000) to a ridge that parallels the San Andreas Rift Zone in San Bernardino National Forest. Next, you hike through some 75 miles of Angeles National Forest, ascending Mt. Baden-Powell (9399) along the way. Finally, you descend through Soledad Canyon on your way to Escondido Canyon and the town of Agua Dulce (2530).

Hike 1—I-15 near Cajon Pass to Swarthout Canyon Road 3N28

PCT: 5.5 miles
Hike: 5.5 miles
Map: D-1 (San Bernardino NF)
Difficulty: Easy

🚶 **Hike.** From the TH (3000), the PCT goes west through the tunnel under I-15 just south of the parking area and crosses Southern Pacific railroad tracks (3020). At 2.4 miles from the TH, you cross Road 3N78 (3360). In another 3.1 miles, you reach your destination, Swarthout Canyon Road 3N28 (3560), which sits right on top of the San Andreas Rift Zone.

🚐 **I-15 near Cajon Pass.** From the Cleghorn/Silverwood Lake exit off Highway 138 near Silverwood Lake, the starting point of the last hike in Section C, go NE 2.4 miles on Highway 138 to Highway 173. Bear left (NW)—stay on Highway 138—and go 8.2 miles to the Cajon Junction exit off Highway I-15. When you reach the east frontage road, turn left (S) and

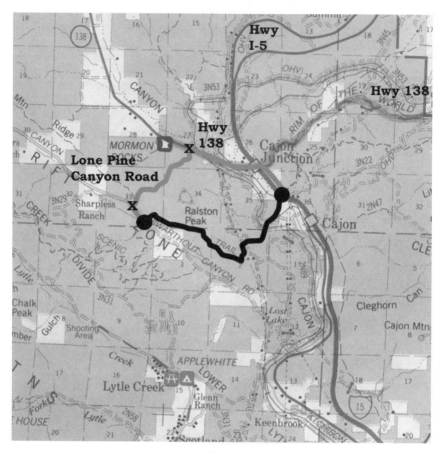

D-1

go 0.5 mile to a parking area near the Santa Fe Trail Pioneers Memorial. The PCT goes west through the tunnel under Highway I-15 just south of the parking area.

🚗 **Swarthout Canyon Road 3N28.** From the east frontage road off I-15 at Cajon Junction, go W 1.2 miles on Highway 138 to Lone Pine Canyon road. Turn left (SW) and go 1.5 miles to Swarthout Canyon road. Turn left (E) road and go 0.4 mile to the PCT. There is a small parking area a few yards past the PCT marker.

(There are other roads that lead to the PCT in this area, but most require high-clearance 4WD. We have selected the roads that are best suited to passenger cars. Furthermore, we have driven to all of the trail-heads in this guide in passenger cars.)

Hike 2—Swarthout Canyon Road 3N28 to Sheep Creek Truck Road 3N31

PCT: 8.6 miles
Hike: 8.6 miles
Map: D-2 (San Bernardino NF)
Difficulty: Easy

🚶 **Hike.** This is an excellent hike as you climb up from Swarthout Canyon Road 3N28 (3560) to, and eventually traverse, Upper Lytle Creek Ridge, with great views of Lytle Creek Canyon to the south and Lone Pine Canyon to the north. At 4.4 miles into the hike, you cross Sharpless Ranch Road 3N29 (5150), then continue another 4.2 miles to your destination, Sheep Creek Truck Road 3N31 (6300).

🚗 **Sheep Creek Truck Road 3N31.** Retrace your route to Lone Pine Canyon road. Turn left (W) and go 3.7 miles to FR 3N31. Turn left (S) and go 2.9 miles to the ridge, a road junction, and the PCT. There is a small parking area at the junction. There is no PCT post on the north side of FR 3N31, but the trail is obvious.

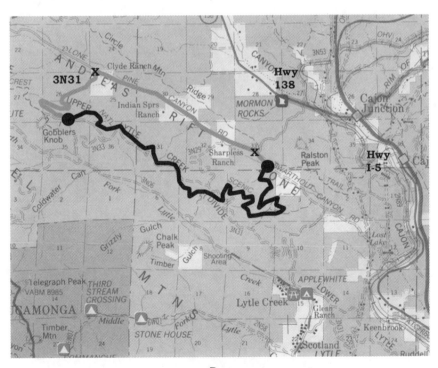

D-2

Hike 3—Sheep Creek Truck Road 3N31 to Inspiration Point

PCT: 13.1 miles
Hike: 13.1 miles
Map: D-3 (Angeles NF)
Difficulty: Moderate

🚶 **Hike.** From Sheep Creek Truck Road 3N31 (6300), this hike follows Upper Lytle Creek Ridge 5.4 miles to a jeep road atop Blue Ridge (8115). From here, you hike 1.7 miles to the Acorn Canyon trail (8250) west of Wright Mountain. In another 0.9 mile you enter the Guffy CG (8225). In the last 5.1 miles to Angeles Crest Highway 2 and Inspiration Point (7386), you pass Holiday Hill ski lift, Blue Ridge Camp, and Blue Ridge ski lifts.

🚙 **Inspiration Point.** Retrace your route to Lone Pine Canyon road. Turn left (W) and go 3.9 miles to Highway 2 near Wrightwood. Turn left (W) and go 4.6 miles to the junction of Highway 2 and Big Pine Highway (N4). Bear left (W)—stay on Highway 2—and go 1.8 miles to Inspiration Point.

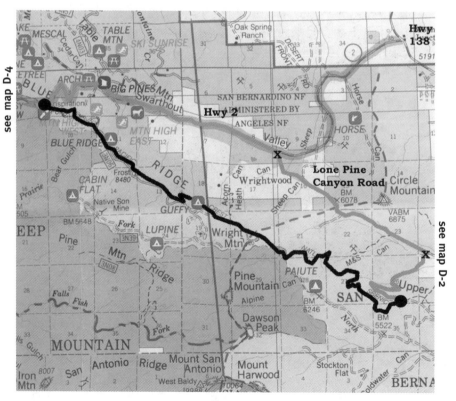

D-3

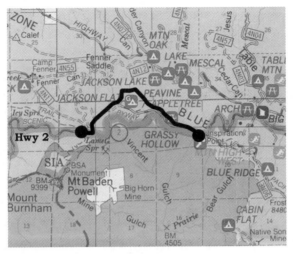

D-4

Hike 4—Inspiration Point to Vincent Gap

PCT: 4.6 miles
Hike: 4.6 miles
Map: D-4 (Angeles NF)
Difficulty: Moderate

Hike. This is a short, but compelling, exposure to the PCT. The hike proceeds W 1.0 mile to the Grassy Hollow Family CG (7300), then 1.3 miles to the Jackson Flat Group CG (7480). You cross Road 3N26 (7220) 1.5 miles further. Then it is a short 0.8-mile descent back to Highway 2 at Vincent Gap (6585).

Vincent Gap. From Inspiration Point, go W 3.2 miles on Highway 2 to Vincent Gap, which affords ample parking and great views.

Hike 5—Vincent Gap to Islip Saddle

PCT: 11.6 miles
Hike: 11.6 miles
Map: D-5 (Angeles NF)
Difficulty: Difficult

Hike. This hike climbs steeply from Vincent Gap (6585) 3.8 miles to the Mt. Baden Powell Spur Trail (9245). The PCT continues W 5.2 miles along this high ridge past Mt. Burnham and Throop Peak, before descending to Windy Gap (7588). It is another 2.6 miles, past the Little Jimmy CG (7450) to Highway 2 just east of Islip Saddle (6670). Check conditions before you go, as snow may linger on these steep slopes until July.

Islip Saddle. From Vincent Gap, go W 10.6 miles on Highway 2 to Islip Saddle.

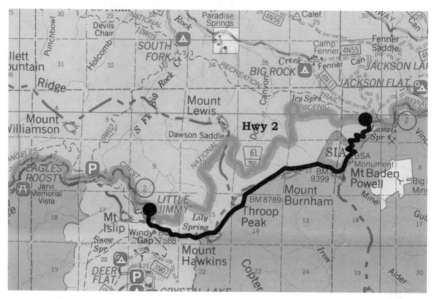

D-5

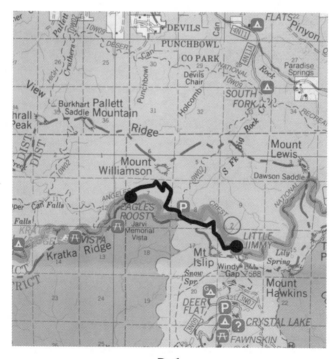

D-6

Hike 6—Islip Saddle to Eagles Roost

PCT: 3.8 miles
Hike: 3.8 miles
Map: D-6 (Angeles NF)
Difficulty: Easy

Hike. This is another short, enjoyable, level hike, one with easy access points at each end. It is 1.6 miles from Islip Saddle (6670) to the Mt. Williamson Summit Trail (7900). In another 1.3 miles, you cross Highway 2 (6700). You reach Highway 2 again 0.9 mile further at Eagles Roost Picnic Area (6650).

Eagles Roost. From Islip Saddle, go W 2.3 miles on Highway 2 to Eagle Roost.

Hike 7—Eagles Roost to Cloudburst Summit

PCT: 7.0 miles
Hike: 7.0 miles
Map: D-7 (Angeles NF)
Difficulty: Moderate

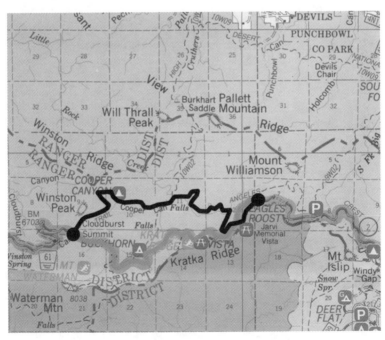

D-7

Hike. This hike dips from Eagles Roost 1.5 miles into Rattlesnake Canyon, where it crosses Little Rock Creek (6080). It follows this creek 2.3 miles to Burkhart Trail 10W02 (5640), then begins its 3.2-mile climb through Cooper Canyon to Cloudburst Summit (7018).

Cloudburst Summit. Go W 4.6 miles from Eagles Roost on Highway 2 to Cloudburst Summit.

Hike 8—Cloudburst Summit to Three Points

PCT: 4.7 miles
Hike: 4.7 miles
Map: D-8 (Angeles NF)
Difficulty: Easy

Hike. Another short but scenic hike along Highway 2, which descends 4.7 miles from Cloudburst Summit (7018) to Three Points (5885).

Three Points. Go W 4.3 miles from Cloudburst on Highway 2 to FR 3N17 and the Three Points TH parking area.

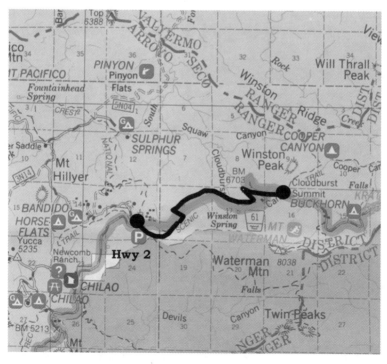

D-8

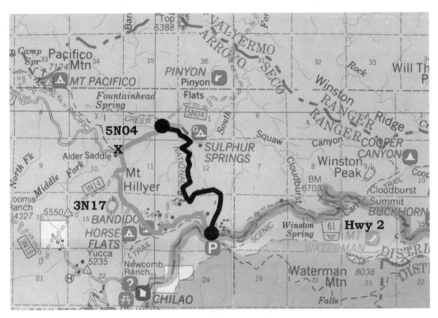

D-9

Hike 9—Three Points to Little Rock Creek Road 5N04

PCT: 4.1 miles
Hike: 4.1 miles
Map: D-9 (Angeles NF)
Difficulty: Easy

Hike. Another short, enjoyable hike. From Three Points (5885), the PCT descends gradually 3.3 miles to the Sulphur Springs CG (5200). It is another 0.8 mile to Little Rock Creek Road 5N04 (5320).

Little Rock Creek Road 5N04. From the junction of Highway 2 and FR 3N17 near the Three Points TH, go W 3.7 miles on paved FR 3N17 to unsigned FR 5N04. There is a sign at the intersection that reads ANGE-LES CREST HIGHWAY 4, ANGELES FOREST HIGHWAY 8. Stay on the paved road to the right—it becomes FR 5N04. Go N 1.0 mile to the PCT, where 5N04 branches to the Sulphur Springs CG. The paved road ends in 0.1 mile. You can park here and walk back to the PCT.

Hike 10—Little Rock Creek Road 5N04 to Mill Creek Summit

PCT: 11.5 miles
Hike: 11.5 miles
Map: D-10 (Angeles NF)
Difficulty: Moderate

Hike. The hike from Little Rock Creek Road 5N04 (5320) parallels Road 3N17 as it winds west 5.9 miles along several ridges to a shady gap (6645) near the Pacifico Mountain CG. You descend gradually through the same kind of terrain for 5.6 miles, finally arriving at Mill Creek Summit (4910).

Mill Creek Summit—from the east, preferred option. Retrace your route to the junction of FRs 3N17/5N04 and the sign that reads ANGELES CREST HIGHWAY 4, ANGELES FOREST HIGHWAY 8. Turn right (W) on FR 3N17, now a dirt road, and go 7.6 miles to the Mill Creek Summit Ranger Station and a TH parking area. (FR 3N17 is closed from here to Mill Creek Summit from November 15 to May 15, and at other times at the discretion of the USFS.)

Mill Creek Summit—from the east, longer paved option. You can use this paved option if FR 3N17 is closed. (This route is not shown on Map D-10.) Retrace your route to Highway 2. Turn right (W) on Highway 2 and go 10.1 miles to Upper Big Tujunga Canyon road. Turn right (NW) and go 9.1 miles to Angeles Forest Highway. Turn right (N) and go 6.2 miles to Mill Creek Summit. Follow the sign at the summit E 0.2 mile to FR 3N17 and the TH parking area.

Mill Creek Summit at FR 59—from the west. From Highway 14 south of Palmdale, take the Angeles Forest Highway exit (FR 59) and go S 10.0 miles to Mill Creek Summit.

View near Mill Creek Summit

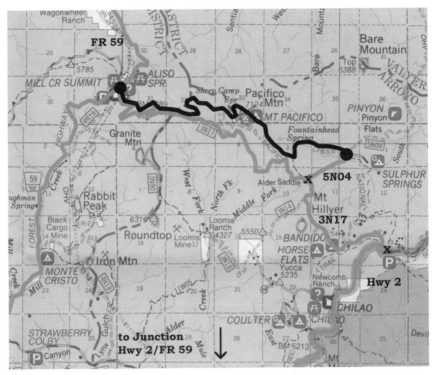

D-10

Hike 11—Mill Creek Summit to Messenger Flats CG

PCT: 11.8 miles
Hike: 11.8 miles
Map: D-11 (Angeles NF)
Difficulty: Moderate

Hike. From Mill Creek Summit (4910), the PCT parallels Mt. Gleason Road 3N17 as it winds W 11.8 miles along several ridges, finally ending at the Messenger Flats CG (5870). The PCT crosses this road several times on its journey west.

Messenger Flats CG. From Mill Creek Summit, go west on paved FR 3N17 (Mt. Gleason road). At the end of 6.2 miles, the pavement ends as you pass the entrance to State Prison Camp #16. Bear left—stay on FR 3N17—and go 3.9 miles to the Messenger Flats CG. The PCT crosses 3N17 there.

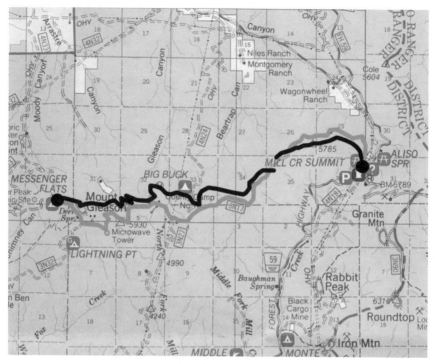

D-11

Hike 12—Messenger Flats CG to Soledad Canyon Road

PCT: 14.2 miles
Hike: 14.2 miles
Map: D-12 (Angeles NF)
Difficulty: Moderate
Direction: S→N (Elevation)

Hike. From the Messenger Flats CG (5870), this hike descends W 5.5 miles to Road 4N32 (4210) near North Fork Saddle Ranger Station. Here the PCT turns N and continues its descent 4.3 miles to Mattox Canyon creek (2685). It is another 4.4 miles to Soledad Canyon Road (2237).

Soledad Canyon Road—from the east. From the Messenger Flats CG, turn left (W) on dirt FR 3N17 and go 1.4 miles to FR 4N33. (From this junction, you could follow 4N33 down to Soledad road, but this dirt road is rough and not well-marked. Furthermore, you would miss some spectacular ridges on the route we recommend.) So, at the junction of FRs 3N17/4N33, stay on FR 3N17 (now marked FR 3N1716) and go W 7.0 miles to North Fork Ranger Station. Continue west on now partially

paved 3N17 4.3 miles to Indian Canyon Road 4N37. Turn right (N) and
go 5.5 miles to Soledad Canyon road where the PCT crosses it.

🚗 **Soledad Canyon Road—from the west**. From Highway 14 south
of Palmdale, take the Soledad Canyon road exit. Go W 10.1 miles through
the town of Acton (not shown on Map D-12) to Indian Canyon Road
4N37 and the PCT.

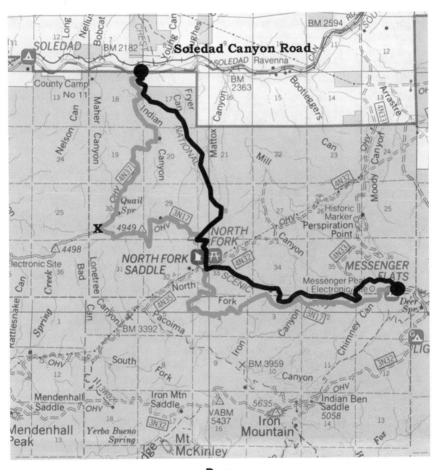

D-12

Hike 13—Soledad Canyon Road to Agua Dulce

PCT: 9.7 miles
Hike: 9.7 miles
Map: D-13 (Angeles NF)
Difficulty: Moderate

Hike. This hike gets high marks because the last 1.5 miles pass through the spectacular Vasquez Rocks County Park. After leaving Soledad Canyon road, you quickly ford the Santa Clara River (2205) and cross Southern Pacific tracks (2243) before reaching a trio of power lines and Young Canyon road (2960). You are now 2.1 miles from where you started. The PCT turns NW for 4.9 miles to a tunnel under Antelope Valley Highway 14 (2370) in Escondido Valley. It is 1.9 miles from Highway 14 to Escondido Canyon road (2510). Most of that distance is spent in the County Park. From the park entrance, hike W 0.3 mile along Escondido Canyon road to a stop sign and Agua Dulce Canyon road (2470). Go N 0.5 mile on Agua Dulce Canyon road to the center of Agua Dulce (2530), the post office, and a general store.

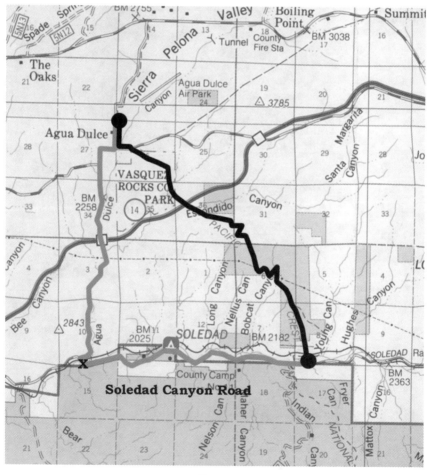

D-13

�"🚗" **Agua Dulce**. From the junction of Indian Canyon road, Soledad Canyon road, and the PCT, go W 4.0 miles on Soledad Canyon road to Agua Dulce Canyon road. Turn right (N) and go 2.2 miles to Highway 14. Go under the freeway and continue N 1.8 miles to a stop sign at the junction of Agua Dulce Canyon road and Escondido Canyon road. There is a PCT marker on the south side of the road. To park at Vasquez Rocks County Park, continue straight (E) and go 0.3 mile on Escondido Canyon road to the park entrance. To get to the center of Agua Dulce (2530) from the stop sign, turn left (N)—stay on Agua Dulce Canyon Road—and go 0.5 mile to the post office and general store.

Agua Dulce to Highway 58 near Mojave

Overview

PCT: 108.8 miles
Day Hikes (9): 108.8 miles
Declination: 13.75° E

From the town of Agua Dulce (2530), Section E of the PCT climbs through the western portion of Angeles National Forest. Near Liebre Mountain (5720), it is forced by private-property constraints exercised by Tejon Ranch to descend into the Mojave Desert near Highway 138 (3040). The ranch refuses to grant permission to build a trail through its property which would be true to the crest and much more desirable. Rather, we are faced with a long, dry, dangerous trek across the desert and up to Oak Creek Canyon, eventually reaching Tehachapi Pass (3830). The excitement in the last few miles of the hike is the hundreds of windmills you pass along the way.

Hike 1—Agua Dulce to Bouquet Canyon Road

PCT: 10.3 miles
Hike: 10.3 miles
Map: E-1 (Angeles NF)
Difficulty: Moderate

Hike. From the town of Agua Dulce (2530) hike N 1.8 miles on Agua Dulce Canyon road, following PCT signs on the side of the road, to Sierra Highway (2725). Cross the highway and proceed N 5.3 miles up the east side of Mint Canyon to Pelona Ridge Road 6N07 (4500). From here, it is 3.2 miles through Martindale Canyon to Bouquet Canyon road (3340).

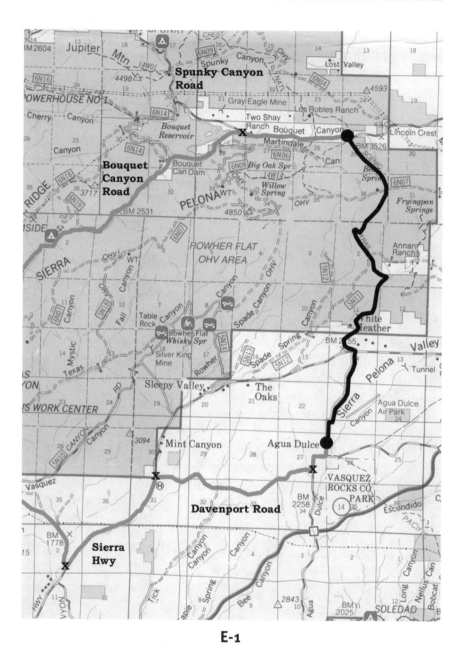

E-1

🚐 **Agua Dulce**. From the junction of Indian Canyon road, Soledad Canyon road, and the PCT, where the last hike in Section D began, go W 4.0 miles on Soledad Canyon road to Agua Dulce Canyon road. Turn right (N) and go 2.2 miles to Highway 14. Go under the freeway and continue N 1.8 miles to a stop sign at the junction of Agua Dulce Canyon road and Escondido Canyon road. There is a PCT marker on the south side of the road. To park at Vasquez Rocks County Park, continue straight (E) and go 0.3 mile on Escondido Canyon road to the park entrance. To get to the center of Agua Dulce (2530) from the stop sign, turn left (N)—stay on Agua Dulce Canyon road—and go 0.5 mile to the post office and general store.

Bouquet Canyon Road. From the center of Agua Dulce, retrace your route S 0.5 mile to the stop sign at the junction of Agua Dulce road and Escondido road. Turn right (W) on Agua Dulce Canyon road and go 0.5 mile to Davenport road. Turn right (W) and go 3.6 miles to Sierra Highway. Turn left (SW) and go 2.7 miles to Vasquez Canyon road. Turn right (W) and go 3.6 miles to Bouquet Canyon road. Turn right (N) and go 11.5 miles to the junction of Bouquet Canyon road and Spunky Canyon road. Bear right (E) on Bouquet Canyon road and go 2.1 miles to the PCT.

Hike 2—Bouquet Canyon Road to San Francisquito Canyon Road

PCT: 12.4 miles
Hike: 12.4 miles
Map: E-2 (Angeles NF)
Difficulty: Moderate

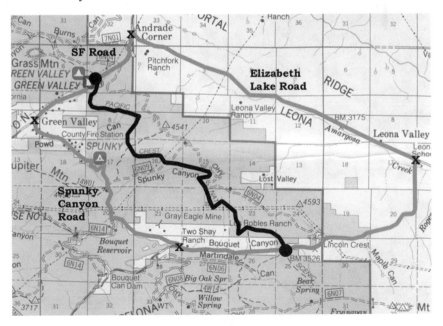

E-2

Hike. This hike parallels Elizabeth Lake road as it winds through Spunky Canyon on its way to Green Valley. From Bouquet Canyon road (3340), the PCT climbs gradually NW 6.1 miles to Road 6N09 in Spunky Canyon (3725). From here, it zigs and zags 6.3 miles to San Francisquito road (3385) near Green Valley Ranger Station.

San Francisquito Canyon Road—option 1. From the Bouquet Canyon road TH, retrace your route 2.1 miles to the junction of Bouquet Canyon road and Spunky Canyon road. Bear right (NW) on Spunky Canyon road and go 5.3 miles to San Francisquito Canyon road. Turn right (NE) and go 1.5 miles to the Green Valley Ranger Station, where you can park. The PCT is 0.1 mile north of the Ranger Station.

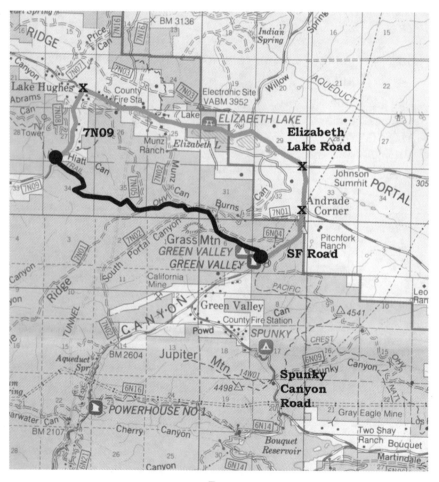

E-3

🚗 **San Franciscquito Canyon Road—option 2**. From the Bouquet Canyon road TH, go E 4.3 miles on Bouquet Canyon road to Elizabeth Lake road. Turn left (W) and go 6.6 miles to San Franciscquito road. Turn left (S) and go 1.4 miles to the PCT. You can park 0.1 mile south at the Green Valley Ranger Station.

Hike 3—San Franciscquito Canyon Road to Lake Hughes Road 7N09

PCT: 7.6 miles
Hike: 7.6 miles
Map: E-3 (Angeles NF)
Difficulty: Easy

🚶 **Hike**. From the TH (3385), hike NW 2.9 miles up to a saddle (3900) on the north slope of Grass Mountain. Continue W 4.7 miles down to Lake Hughes Road 7N09 (3050).

🚗 **Lake Hughes Road 7N09**. From San Franciscquito Canyon road, retrace your route to Elizabeth Lake road. Turn left (N) and go 0.8 mile to the junction of Elizabeth Lake road and Johnson road. Turn left (W) on Elizabeth Lake road and go 4.5 miles to Lake Hughes Road 7N09. Turn left (SW) and go 1.4 miles to a parking area on the west side of the road. The PCT is 0.1 mile further south on Lake Hughes road. (At the junction of Lake Hughes road and Elizabeth Lake road, Elizabeth Lake road becomes Pine Canyon road.)

Hike 4—Lake Hughes Road 7N09 to Burnt Peak Road

PCT: 9.6 miles
Hike: 9.6 miles
Map: E-4 (Angeles NF)
Difficulty: Easy

🚶 **Hike**. This is a pleasant hike along the Sawmill Mountains to a vista near Burnt Peak. From the Lake Hughes Road 7N09 TH (3050), hike W 3.7 miles up to Maxwell Truck Trail 7N08 (4505). Continue 5.9 miles along Sawmill Mountain Ridge to the junction of Burnt Peak road, FR 7N23, and the PCT (5245).

🚗 **Burnt Peak Road**. Retrace your route to the junction of Elizabeth Lake road to the east and Pine Canyon road to the west. (This is an interesting intersection because the same east-west road changes names

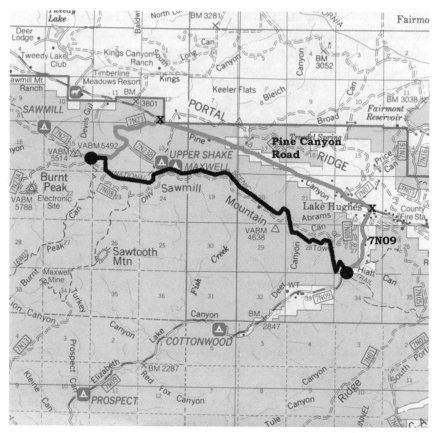

E-4

where it intersects Lake Hughes road.) Turn left (W) on Pine Canyon road
and go 4.7 miles to dirt FR 7N23. Turn left (S) and go 3.0 miles to the
ridge-top intersection of the PCT, FR 7N23, and usually closed Burnt
Peak Road 7N23A.

Hike 5—Burnt Peak Road to Pine Canyon Road

PCT: 14.5 miles
Hike: 14.5 miles
Map: E-5 (Angeles NF)
Difficulty: Moderate

Hike. This hike proceeds W 3.4 miles along the Sawmill Mountain
Ridge, paralleling Road 7N23, to Atmore Meadows Spur Road 7N19
(4705). It continues W 4.3 miles, still paralleling Road 7N23, to a spur trail
(5370) that leads to the Bear CG. Continue W 2.4 miles to a dirt road

(5720) near Liebre Mountain where the PCT jogs north. Go N 4.4 miles as you descend along Horse Camp Canyon to Pine Canyon road [Highway N2 (3845)] and leave Angeles National Forest.

🚗 **Pine Canyon Road**. Retrace your route to Pine Canyon road. Turn left (W) and go 4.8 miles to the junction of Pine Canyon road and Three Points road. Turn left (W) on Pine Canyon road (Highway N2) and go 2.8 miles to the PCT. (The NF map incorrectly identifies Three Points road from Highway 138 to Three Points as Pine Canyon road.)

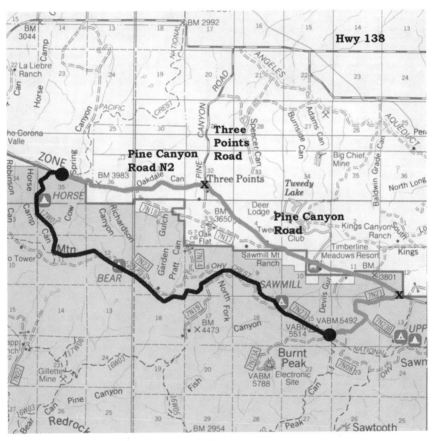

E-5

Hike 6—Pine Canyon Road to Highway 138 at 269th Street

PCT: 6.7 miles
Hike: 6.7 miles
Map: E-6 (Angeles NF)
Difficulty: Easy

Hike. From Pine Canyon road [Highway N2 (3845)], this hike passes N 6.7 miles through Tejon Ranch. Signs warn you to stay on the trail. As the Schaffer guide says, this is a "tiring and annoying stretch of the trail." It ends on Highway 138 at 269th Street (3040).

Highway 138 at 269th Street. Retrace your route on Highway N2 to the junction of Pine Canyon road and Three Points road. Turn left (N) on Three Points and go N 3.0 miles to Highway 138 (Lancaster road). Turn left (W) and go 0.9 mile to 269th Street, where the PCT crosses Highway 138. (The NF map incorrectly identifies Three Points road from Highway 138 to Three Points as Pine Canyon road.)

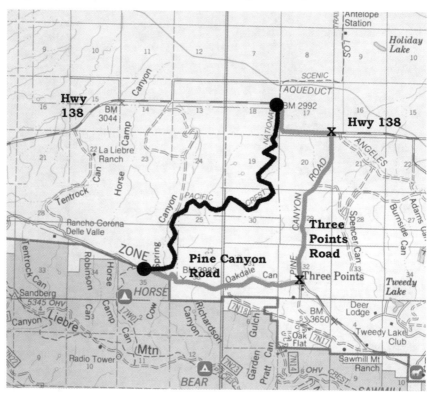

E-6

Hike 7—Highway 138 at 269th Street to Cottonwood Creek Bridge

PCT: 16.4 miles
Hike: 16.4 miles
Map: E-7 (Angeles NF)
Difficulty: Moderate

Hike. This level, hot, dry, dangerous hike starts at Highway 138 and 269th Street (3040). It plows through the desert, often on dry, dirt roads. It follows the Los Angeles Aqueduct part of the way before arriving 16.4 miles later at the Cottonwood Creek Bridge (3120).

Cottonwood Creek. From 269th Street, go E 9.9 miles on Highway 138 to 170th Street. Turn left (N) and go 6.0 miles to Rosamond Boulevard. At this junction, Rosamond turns east, but you go north on the dirt road, a continuation of 170th Street, 1.5 miles to the sign for BROKEN ARROW ROAD. Follow the "Broken Arrow" arrow to the left (NW) and go 1.7 miles to the PCT. (The concrete bridge over Cottonwood Creek is 0.2 mile south of this PCT sign.) The road and the PCT are one and the same for the next 0.4 mile west, at which juncture the PCT leaves the road to begin its journey north.

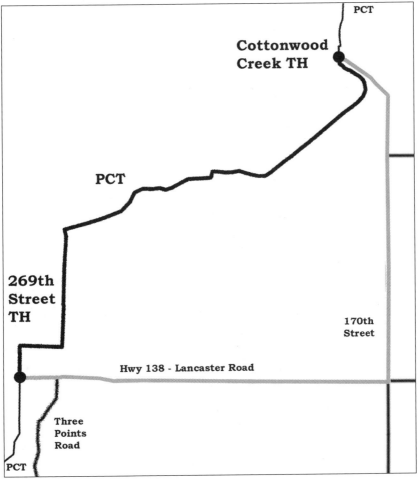

E-7

Hike 8—Cottonwood Creek Bridge to Tehachapi-Willow Springs Road

PCT: 22.7 miles
Hike: 22.7 miles
Maps: E-8A and E-8B
Difficulty: Difficult
Direction: N→S (Elevation)

Hike. From Cottonwood Creek (3120), you climb N 6.6 miles out of the desert to a ridge above Tylerhorse Canyon (4960). Zig and zag E 3.9 miles to Gamble Springs Canyon (4625). From here, you climb N 3.0 miles to a jeep road (6070) near the top of the ridge. From here you go NE 2.6

continued on map E-8B

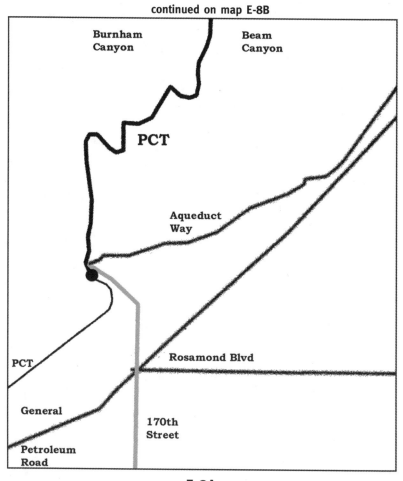

E-8A

miles to a gap at the heads of Burnham and Pitney canyons (5980), then descend 6.6 miles to Oak Creek (4075) and Tehachapi-Willow Springs road (4150). The last few miles of this hike are awesome as you wind your way through a world of wind farms and windmills. (Be sure to take plenty of water as this hike is strenuous and temperatures can easily climb into triple digits from late spring through early fall.)

🚗 **Tehachapi-Willow Springs Road**. From Cottonwood Creek, return to Rosamond and 170th. Turn left (E) on Rosamond and go 8.0 miles to Tehachapi-Willow Springs road. Turn left (N) and go 14.3 miles to Cameron road. The PCT crosses Tehachapi-Willow Springs road a few yards east of Cameron road.

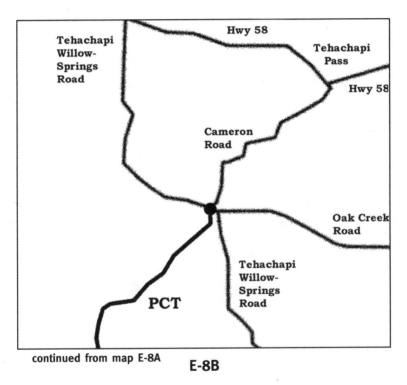

continued from map E-8A   **E-8B**

Hike 9—Tehachapi-Willow Springs Road to Highway 58 near Tehachapi Pass

PCT: 8.6 miles
Hike: 8.6 miles
Map: E-9
Difficulty: Moderate

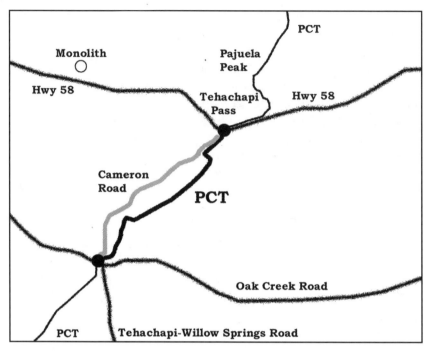

E-9

🚶 **Hike**. This hike gets high marks because it is easy to access at both ends, and because there are so many windfarms in the hills as you wind your way above Cameron Canyon to Tehachapi Pass. From Tehachapi-Willow Springs road (4150) climb moderately NE 2.2 miles to a ridgetop (4560) where you can see windfarms, the desert, and mountains in the distance to the south. You cross another dirt road (4485) 1.6 miles further, then continue 3.5 miles down to Cameron road (3905), which you follow 1.3 miles across railroad tracks and then across Highway 58 (3830) to the end of Section E.

🚗 **Highway 58 near Tehachapi Pass**. From Oak Creek Canyon, go N 5.4 miles on Cameron road to Highway 58. The PCT crosses Highway 58 at the Cameron road exit near Tehachapi Pass. You can park on the north side of the road. (If you are coming from the east, find the junction of Highways 14/58 north of the town of Mojave, then go west on Highway 14 to the Cameron road exit.)

Highway 58 near Tehachapi Pass to Highway 178 at Walker Pass

Overview

PCT: 66.8 miles
Day Hikes (5): 84.2 mile
PCT Inaccessible to Day Hikes: 17.3 miles
Declination: 13.75° E

Welcome to the Sierra Nevada! From the Cameron road overpass over Highway 58 near Tehachapi Pass (3830), the PCT climbs to the Sierra crest (6170), where it remains for most of Section F. It is a pleasant area to hike, and you will be amazed at the different ecosystems you will encounter along the way. In the middle of Section F, you hike above Kelso Valley, which is both beautiful and virtually unknown to most, before arriving at Bird Spring Pass (5355). Shortly thereafter, you reach Highway 178 at Walker Pass (5246).

The beginning of this section was a logistical nightmare. The only way to break the first 34.7 miles into two pieces involved some heavy-duty 4WD. We decided not to include the 4WD option because (a) there are several gates along the way that may be locked, (b) some of the jeep trails are on private property, (c) this fragile ecosystem does not need any more 4WD than it already gets, and (d) we had decided to use only roads passable to passenger cars. Rather, we describe two round-trip day hikes that let you sample the beginning and end of this stretch of the trail. Of course, it is possible to backpack this stretch, but horse travel is not advised because there are some very treacherous parts with steep cliffs on both sides.

If you plan to hike in this area, be sure to stop at the Bureau of Land Management (BLM) Jawbone Station, 28111 Jawbone Canyon Road, P. O. Box D, Cantil, CA 93519, Phone: (760) 373-1146. This is one of the most helpful offices we have encountered anywhere in our travels along the

PCT. They understand and practice the concept of "service." Not only can you obtain maps and guides to the area, they will be glad to help you get just about anywhere you would like to go. They may even be able to identify local residents who can help you arrange your hikes along the PCT.

Hike 1—Highway 58 near Tehachapi Pass to the Head of Waterfall Canyon

PCT: 8.3 miles
Hike: 16.6 miles
Map: F-1
Difficulty: Moderate
Direction: S→N (Round Trip)

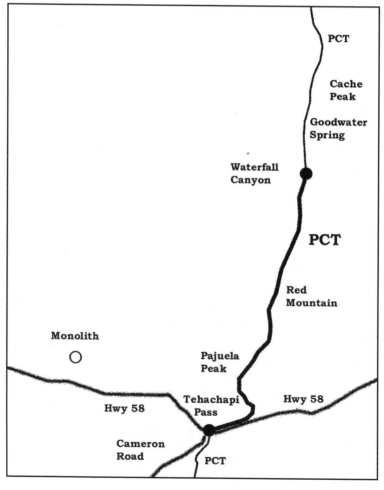

F-1

🚶 **Hike**. This is a rigorous hike. From the Cameron overpass over Highway 58 near Tehachapi Pass (3830), hike E 1.2 miles to a gate (3780). From here it is up, steeply at first, then more gradually until you reach the head of Waterfall Canyon (6120), 7.1 miles from where you began your ascent at the gate. Views from the top of the ridge are spectacular, not to mention the plethora of windmills that dot the landscape. The head of Waterfall Canyon is your turn-around point for the hike back down to Highway 58.

🚗 **Highway 58 near Tehachapi Pass**. From Oak Creek Canyon, the starting point for the last hike in Section E, go N 5.4 miles on Cameron road to Highway 58. The PCT crosses Highway 58 at the Cameron road exit near Tehachapi Pass. You can park on the north side of the road. (If you are coming from the east, find the junction of Highways 14/58 north of Mojave, then go W on Highway 14 to the Cameron road exit.)

(The 17.3 PCT miles between the head of Waterfall Canyon and the Miller Springs Jeep Road where Hike 2 ends are miles we have defined as "inaccessible" to day hikers.)

Hike 2—Jawbone Canyon Road near Geringer Grade to Miller Springs Jeep Road

PCT: 9.1 miles
Hike: 18.2 miles
Map: F-2
Difficulty: Moderate
Direction: N→S (Round Trip)

🚶 **Hike**. This is a round-trip hike that, by necessity, begins at its north end. Hence, we describe it N→S. From Jawbone road near Geringer Grade (6620), hike S 5.8 miles, past Robin Bird Spring and around Weldon Peak, to Hamp Williams Pass (5530). From here, you descend S 3.3 miles to the jeep road (5010) that leads west to Miller Springs, your turn-around point.

🚗 **Jawbone Canyon Road near Geringer Grade**. Find Highway 14 north of the town of Mojave. Go north on Highway 14 to Jawbone Canyon road and the Jawbone OHV Information Center. Stop by and say "hello" to these friendly folks. Go W 18.1 miles on Jawbone Canyon road. The first 4 miles of this road are paved. The remainder is dirt, but sometimes there are washouts. Check with the BLM office before you go. At 18.1 miles, a sign that reads WELDONE/MT. PIUTE greets you. Bear left (W) and go 0.3 mile to north-south Kelso Valley road. Continue W 8.2 miles on

Jawbone Canyon road to the PCT. This dirt road is steep in places, especially the last 3.5 miles as you climb up to the PCT.

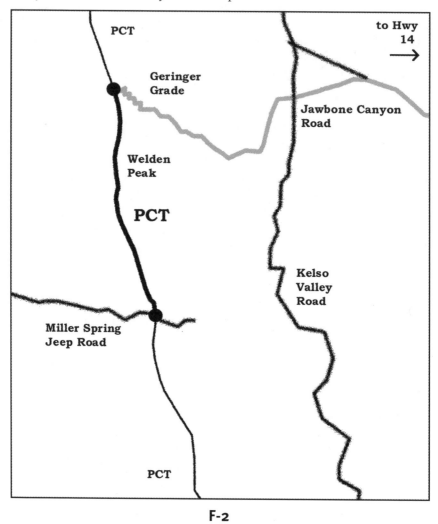

F-2

Hike 3—Jawbone Canyon Road near Geringer Grade to Kelso Valley Road near St. John Ridge

PCT: 13.4 miles
Hike: 13.4 miles
Map: F-3 (Sequoia NF)
Difficulty: Moderate

Hike. We now return to our standard way of describing hikes along the PCT, S→N. This hike, in the Piute Mountains, crosses Piute

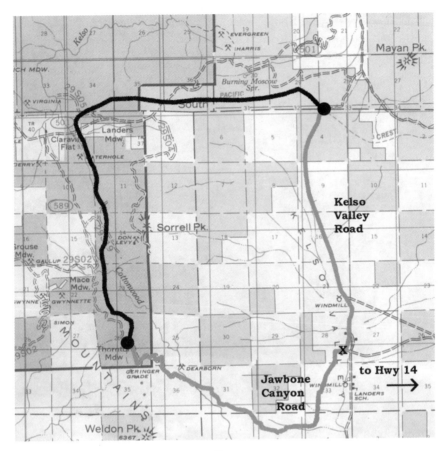

F-3

Mountain road twice as it proceeds to a ridge over beautiful Kelso Valley. From Jawbone Canyon road near Geringer Grade (6620), hike N 1.8 miles to a footbridge over Cottonwood Creek (6480). Continue N 2.9 miles to Landers Creek (6300), and another 0.9 mile N to your first crossing of Piute Mountain road (6220). Go N 0.7 mile to a jeep road (6300), where you turn W for 2.3 miles to the second crossing of Piute Mountain road (6620) at the summit of Harris Grade. Continue W 4.8 miles, descending along St. John Ridge, to Kelso Valley road (4953) at a pass near St. John Mine.

Kelso Valley Road near St. John Ridge—from Jawbone Canyon Road near Geringer Grade. Retrace your route E 8.2 miles on Jawbone Canyon road to Kelso Valley road (dirt). Turn left (N) on Kelso Valley road and go 5.4 miles to where the PCT crosses it.

Kelso Valley Road near St. John Ridge—from Highway 14. From the junction of Highway 14 and Jawbone Canyon road, go W 18.4 miles on Jawbone road (the first 4 miles are paved; the remainder is dirt) to Kelso Valley road (dirt). Turn right (N) on Kelso Valley road and go 5.4 miles to where the PCT crosses it.

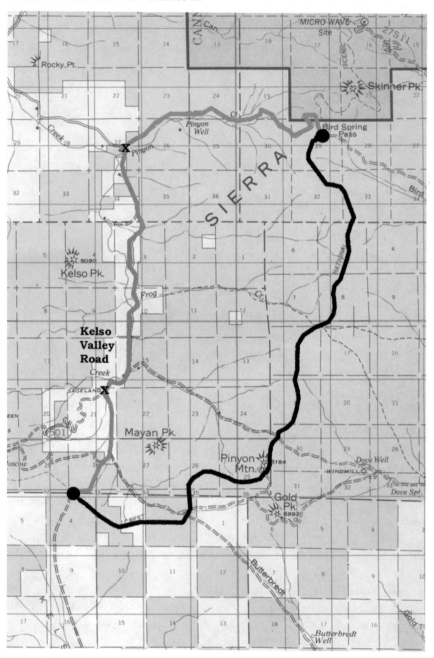

F-4

Hike 4—Kelso Valley Road near St. John Ridge to Bird Spring Pass

PCT: 15.4 miles
Hike: 15.4 miles
Map: F-4 (Sequoia NF)
Difficulty: Moderate

Hike. From Kelso Valley road (4953), descend E 2.1 miles to Road SC123 (4540). From here it is a slow, gradual climb W 4.1 miles to a saddle junction (5283) of several trails and roads, including Road SC103, where the PCT turns north. In 1.6 miles, you reach yet another multi-road-and-trail junction (5382). In the next 2.1 miles, you cross two more roads before arriving at Road SC47 (5380). Continue N 3.0 miles to Road SC42 (5740). It is another 2.5 miles north to Bird Spring Pass and Road SC120 (5355).

Bird Spring Pass—from Kelso Valley Road near St. John Mine. From the junction of the PCT and Kelso Valley road, go N 2.5 miles on Kelso Valley road to a junction and a sign that reads PIUTE MOUNTAIN/HIGHWAY 14. Continue N 5.7 miles on Kelso Valley to Bird Spring Canyon road. Turn right (E) on this narrow, sometimes steep, dirt road and go 5.6 miles to Bird Spring Pass.

Bird Spring Pass—from Highway 178 at Walker Pass. From Walker Pass on Highway 178, go W 20.7 miles to paved Kelso Creek road (not shown on Map F-4). Turn left (S) and go 4.5 miles to an intersection with paved Kelso Valley road. Bear left (S) on Kelso Valley road and go 6.2 miles to Bird Spring Canyon road. Turn left (E) on this narrow, sometimes steep, dirt road and go 5.6 miles to Bird Spring Pass. (You may be tempted to take Bird Spring Canyon road east from the pass to Highway 14, or to take it west from Highway 14 to the pass. Curb this urge unless you have a high-clearance 4WD.)

Hike 5—Bird Spring Pass to Highway 178 at Walker Pass

PCT: 20.6 miles
Hike: 20.6 miles
Map: F-5 (Sequoia NF)
Difficulty: Difficult

Hike. From Bird Spring Pass and SC120 (5355), the PCT climbs 3.7 miles to its highest point in Section F (6940). From here you descend around Skinner Peak 2.3 miles to Horse Canyon Road SC65 (6260), then

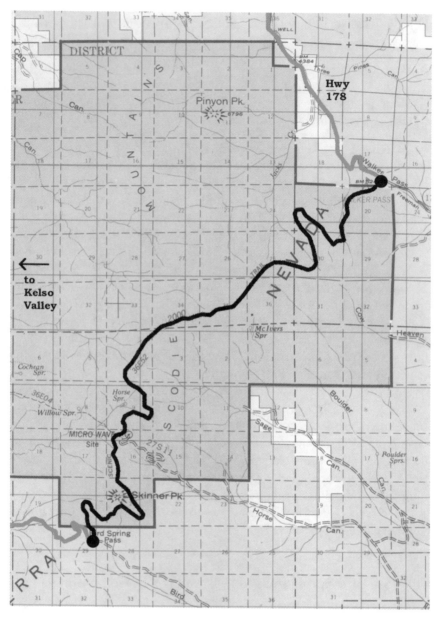

F-5

undulate 4.5 miles to McIvers Spring road (6670). Go NE 2.2 miles to a
fork (6680) where the PCT departs north. From here, you hike 7.3 miles
around the head of Boulder Canyon and then down along Jacks Creek
Canyon, eventually arriving at a path that leads to the Walker Pass TH
CG (5100). It is another 0.6 mile up to Walker Pass and Highway 178
(5246).

🚐 **Highway 178 at Walker Pass—from Bird Spring Pass**. Retrace your route to Kelso Valley road. Turn right (N) and go 6.2 miles to Kelso Creek road (not shown on Map F-5). Bear right (N) on Kelso Creek road and go 4.5 miles to Highway 178. Turn right (E) on Highway 178 and go 20.7 miles to Walker Pass. You can park along Highway 178. There is a historic marker on the south side of the road. The Walker Pass TH CG is 1.0 mile west of the pass on Highway 178.

🚐 **Highway 178 at Walker Pass—from the Freeman Junction of Highways 14/178 near Mojave**. From this junction, go W 8.4 miles on Highway 178 to Walker Pass.

Highway 178 at Walker Pass to Mt. Whitney

Overview

PCT: 71.8 miles
Day Hikes (5): 84.4 miles
PCT Inaccessible to Day Hikes: 41.7 miles
Declination: 14.25° E

The PCT in Section G climbs to the High Sierra, where day hikes are limited. From Olancha Pass, south of Mt. Whitney, to Leavitt Lake, south of Sonora Pass on Highway 108 in Section I, there are few access points. However, we describe several day hikes that take you to spectacular points along the PCT.

Hike 1—Highway 178 at Walker Pass to Canebrake Road near Chimney Creek CG

PCT: 28.3 miles
Hike: 28.3 miles
Map: G-1A (Sequoia NF), G-1B (Sequoia NF)
Difficulty: Difficult

Hike. This is a difficult segment for day hikers. This hike is longer than we like, but once again, private property rights need to be observed. If you must bail out on this hike, there two ways to do so.

One option is Cow Canyon road, which runs W 3.9 miles from near the Joshua Tree Spring spur trail on the PCT to Highway 178 6.7 miles west of Walker Pass. This road is gated and access through private property is not possible. It is only mentioned as a bail-out option in case of an emergency.

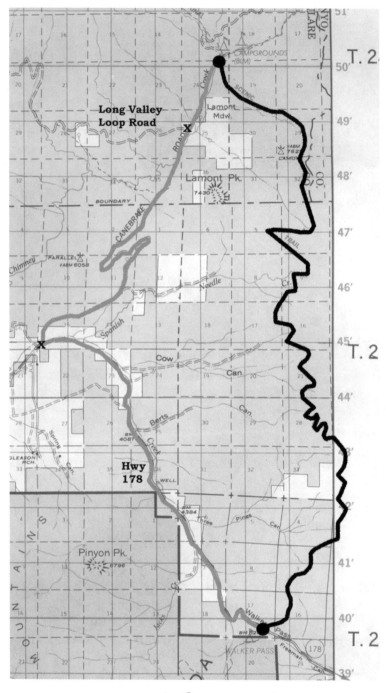

G-1

Another bail-out option is the 4.0-mile jeep trail that leads down Spanish Needle Canyon to Canebrake road. The jeep trail from Canebrake road is now gated and there is a NO TRESPASSING sign posted, so you should consider this option only as an emergency route off the PCT. (Should you need to use this jeep trail and want to tell someone where it comes out, here are the directions: From Walker Pass on Highway 178, go W 9.2 miles to Canebrake road. Turn right (N) on this unpaved road and go 2.5 miles to Spanish Needle Jeep Trail. Turn right. There is a gate as you start your journey east up the trail, and in 0.7 mile, you encounter the locked gate.)

From Walker Pass and Highway 178 (5246), the PCT climbs gradually NE 5.0 miles to Morris/Jenkins saddle (6580), where it turns NW for 6.1 miles to Cow Canyon road (5500), one bail-out option for this hike. In a short 0.4 mile you cross Joshua Tree Spring spur trail (5360). It is another 4.4 miles to headwaters of Spanish Needle Creek (5160), and the Spanish Needle Creek jeep road (5300), your second possible bail-out point. You cross several additional fingers of this creek before arriving in 4.5 miles at a ridge (6800) between the Spanish Needle group and Lamont Peak. Continue E, then N, 3.3 miles to a broad saddle (6900), from which you begin your descent 4.6 miles to Canebrake road (5555).

Highway 178 at Walker Pass—from Bird Spring Pass. From Bird Spring Pass, the starting point for the last hike in Section F, retrace your route to Kelso Valley road. Turn right (N) on Kelso Valley road and go 6.2 miles to Kelso Creek road. Bear right (N) on Kelso Creek road and go 4.5 miles to Highway 178. Turn right (E) and go 20.7 miles to Walker Pass. You can park along Highway 178. There is a historic marker on the south side of the road. The Walker Pass TH CG is 1.0 mile west of the pass on Highway 178.

Highway 178 at Walker Pass—from the Freeman Junction of Highways 14/178 near Mojave. From this junction, go W 8.4 miles on Highway 178 to Walker Pass.

Canebrake Road near Chimney Creek CG—from Highway 178 at Walker Pass. From Walker Pass on Highway 178, go W 9.2 miles to Canebrake road. Turn right (N) on this unpaved road and go 9.0 miles to Long Valley road. Continue straight (N) 1.6 miles on Canebrake road to the PCT. The Chimney Creek CG is 0.2 mile further N.

Canebrake Road near Chimney Creek CG—from Highway 395 north of Freeman Junction. From Highway 395 near the Inyo/Kern County Line, go W 10.6 miles on paved Kennedy Meadows road to Canebrake road. Turn left (S) on Canebrake and go 3.6 miles to the Chimney Creek CG. The PCT crosses Canebrake 0.2 mile further south.

Hike 2—Canebrake Road near Chimney Creek CG to Long Valley Loop Road

PCT: 7.9 miles
Hike: 7.9 miles
Map: G-2 (Sequoia NF)
Difficulty: Easy

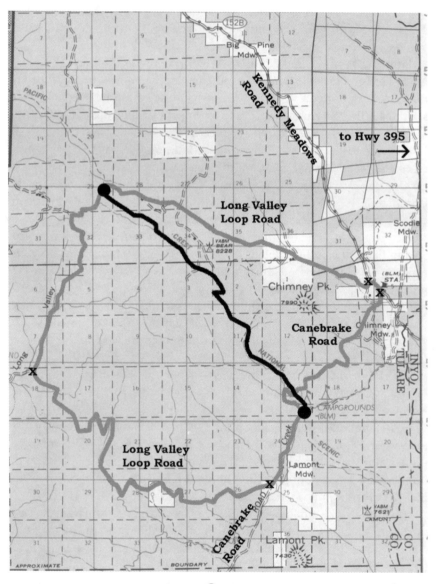

G-2

👤 **Hike.** The PCT proceeds NW 2.2 miles to a dirt road (6580) just past Fox Mill Spring. Continue NW, around Bear Mountain, 3.8 miles to another dirt road (7980), then another 1.9 miles to Long Valley Loop road (7220).

🚗 **Long Valley Loop Road—from Canebrake Road, northerly route.** From where the PCT crosses Canebrake road, go N 4.1 miles on Canebrake (past the Chimney Creek CG) to a Chimney Peak sign and Kennedy Meadows road. (At this sign, you are 10.5 miles west of US Highway 395.) Turn left (NW) on Kennedy Meadows road and go 0.4 mile to the next BLM Chimney Peak sign. Bear left (W) on rough, dirt Long Valley Loop road and go 6.0 miles to the PCT. This road frequently washes out, so be sure to check on its condition before you go.

🚗 **Long Valley Loop Road—from Canebrake Road, southerly route.** From where the PCT crosses Canebrake road, retrace your route 1.6 miles to the signed Long Valley Loop road. Turn right (W) on this rough dirt road and go 9.1 miles to the BLM Long Valley CG. Continue straight on Long Valley Loop road and go 5.0 miles on it to the PCT.

Hike 3—Long Valley Loop Road to Kennedy Meadows CG

PCT: 15.4 miles
Hike: 15.4 miles
Map: G-3 (Sequoia NF)
Difficulty: Moderate

👤 **Hike.** This is a great hike. Proceeding NW 2.7 miles from Long Valley Loop road (7220), you reach a spur ridge (6600) where you enter Dome Land Wilderness and turn north into Rockhouse Basin. You go N 6.0 miles, crossing several creeks that flow into the South Fork Kern River, to a point where the trail meets the river (5760). Continuing N 4.3 miles, you cross Kennedy Meadows road (5950). It is another 2.4 miles, still paralleling the South Fork of the Kern, to the Kennedy Meadows CG (6150).

🚗 **Kennedy Meadows CG.** From the PCT at Long Valley Loop road, go E 6.0 miles to Kennedy Meadows road. Turn left (NW) on Kennedy Meadows road and go 12.9 miles to a sign for the Kennedy Meadows CG and the PCT. Go straight (N) 2.6 miles to the CG and the PCT. The PCT bisects the CG before it departs to the N. There is also a small TH parking area in the middle of the CG. (The Kennedy Meadows General Store is just west of the sign to the Kennedy Meadows CG and the PCT.)

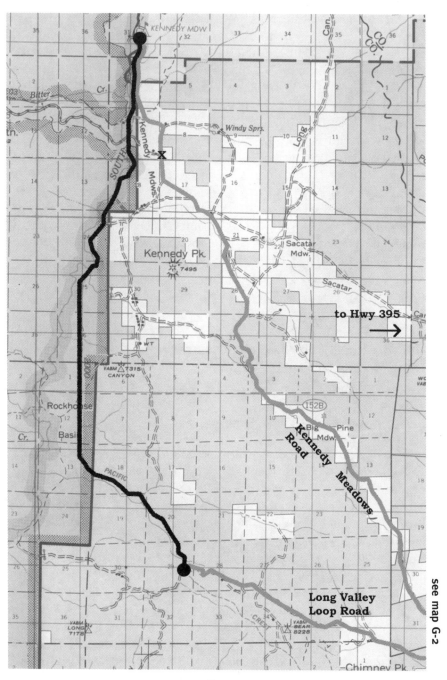

G-3

see map G-2

Northbound PCT sign at Kennedy Meadows TH

Hike 4—Kennedy Meadows CG to Sage Flat Road

PCT: 15.4 miles
Hike: 22.3 miles
Map: G-4 (Sequoia NF)
Difficulty: Difficult

Hike. From the Kennedy Meadows CG (6150), go N 1.9 miles to a bridge over the South Fork Kern River. In another 2.0 miles, you cross Crag Creek (6810). Continue N 2.5 miles through Clover Meadow and along Crag Creek to the Clover Meadow Trail (7560). It is another 5.1 miles to another bridge over the South Fork Kern River (7820). Here you

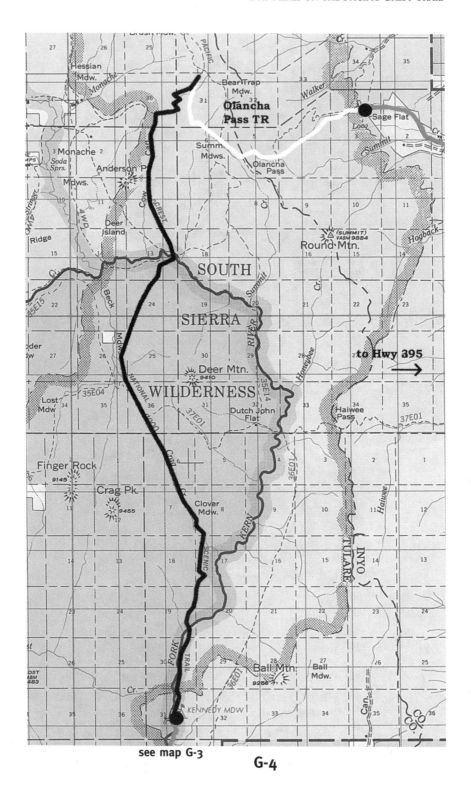

see map G-3

G-4

begin a stretch of 2.7 miles up Cow Canyon to your first of several cross-ings of Cow Creek (8260). You parallel Cow Creek for another 1.2 miles to Olancha Pass Trail 36E02 (8920). You leave the PCT at this point, follow the trail to Olancha Pass, then hike down Trail 36E02 to Sage Flat road. This is a 6.9-mile addition to what you already did on the PCT, but it is the last day hike before reaching many inaccessible miles in the High Sierra.

🚐 **Sage Flat Road and the Olancha Pass TH**. From the Kennedy Meadows CG, retrace your route to Kennedy Meadows road, which you follow E 23.8 miles to Highway 395. Turn left (N) on Highway 395 and go 26.2 miles to Sage Flat road. Turn left (W) on paved Sage Flat road and go 3.2 miles to where the pavement ends. Continue W another 2.2 miles to a corral, parking, and the Olancha Pass TH.

Hike 5—Horseshoe Meadow to Trail Pass to Cottonwood Pass to Horseshoe Meadow

PCT: 4.8 miles
Hike: 10.5 miles
Map: G-5 (Inyo NF)
Difficulty: Moderate
Direction: S→N

🥾 **Hike**. This is a gorgeous hike that takes you out 2.3 miles on the Trail Pass Trail to the PCT (10500) in the High Sierra. You follow the PCT N 4.8 miles to Cottonwood Pass (11160), then return via Cottonwood Pass Trail 3.4 miles to Horseshoe Meadow.

🚐 **Horseshoe Meadow CG and TH**. Retrace your route from the Olancha Pass TH to Highway 395. Turn left (N) on Highway 395 and go 23.8 miles to Lubkin Canyon road. (If you are coming from the north, find the junction of Highways 395/136 south of Lone Pine, then go S 2.5 miles on Highway 395 to Lubkin Canyon road.) Go W 3.3 miles on Lubkin Canyon road to Cottonwood Lakes road. Turn left (S) and follow Cottonwood Lakes road 15.9 miles to the Horseshoe Meadow CG and TH.

Lodging tip in Lone Pine. We recommend the Alabama Hills Inn (760) 876-8700, just south of Lone Pine. They have reasonable rates and a nicely maintained facility.

Golfing tip in Lone Pine. If you like to golf, the Mt. Whitney Golf Club (760) 876-5795 offers exceptional views (Mt. Whitney in the background), exceptional value (less than $30 for 18 holes), and usually a quick round. It is a nine-hole facility with two different sets of tees for each hole.

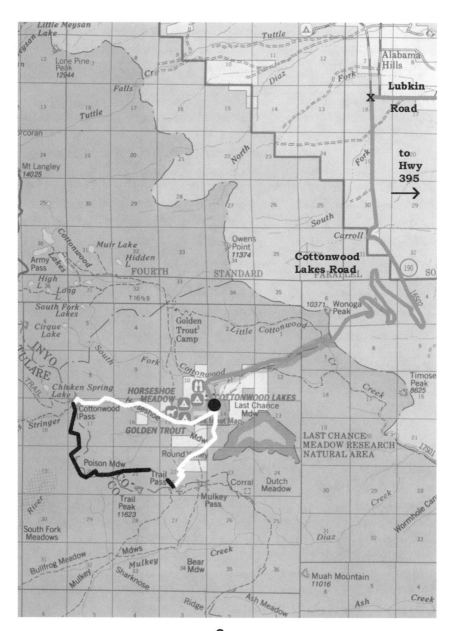

G-5

Mt. Whitney to Tuolumne Meadows

Overview

PCT: 66.3 miles
Hikes (8): 128.8 miles
PCT Inaccessible to Day Hikes: 110.9 miles
Declination: 14° E

S ection H is not highly accessible to day hikers as the PCT winds through the High Sierra. Nevertheless, we describe a few spectacular day hikes, as well as a few places where day hikers can make their way to and from the PCT along scenic routes. This section is further divided into access points on the east and on the west side of the Sierra crest.

Access Points from the East

Overview

If you want a spectacular, one-week introduction to PCT day hikes in the High Sierra, we highly recommend Hikes 1-4 in this section. Three of the hikes are in the Mammoth Lakes region and one is near the town of Independence to the south. Camping and lodging opportunities abound near Mammoth Lakes, but realize that it is a two-hour drive from Mammoth Lakes to Independence.

Assuming you stay in the Mammoth Lakes region, we recommend that you do Hike 2 (Rainbow Falls TH to Agnew Meadows CG) first. It is the shortest (8.0 miles) and there is not much elevation change. If you are up to it, include a side trip to spectacular Rainbow Falls. Second, do Hike 1 (Onion Valley via the Kearsarge Pass Trail to the PCT) as a way to increase your tolerance to high elevation (9000-12000) and to experience hiking up and down hill. Because this is a round-trip hike (6.2 miles each way), you can stop at any point along the way and return to the starting point. The third hike we recommend is Hike 4 (Agnew Meadows CG to Rush Creek TH near Silver Lake CG), which takes you to a spectacular ridge, then down into the June Lake/Silver Lake area. The nice thing

Laurel Mountain in the Mammoth Lakes region

about this hike is that you can make it as short (14.1 miles) or as long (20.4 miles) as you wish. The shortest hike covers 5.2 miles of the PCT and the longest covers 11.0 miles. Finally, save Hike 2 (from the Duck Pass Trail at Coldwater CG to the Rainbow Falls TH) for last. It is a 16.5-mile trek, first up 5.2 miles to the PCT (10150), then down 11.3 miles along the PCT to the Rainbow Falls Trail (7600). These hikes will give you a genuine appreciation of the PCT in the High Sierra. If you take it gradually, the experience can be a great one.

Lodging tips in the Mammoth Lakes area. *There are many places to stay in the Mammoth Lakes region. Our favorite is the Econo Lodge (760) 934-6855; (800) 845-8764, which is owned and operated by the friendly, helpful Patel family They also own the Executive Inn less than a block away, and a new (1999) Holiday Inn. Their rates are reasonable, but most importantly, they are friendly. We will continue to stay with them when we are in the area.*

Dining tips in the Mammoth Lakes area. *There are more than several places to eat in the Mammoth Lakes region. We have two favorites. The first is a gourmet's delight, the Restaurant at Convict Lake (760) 934-3803. Located four miles south of Mammoth Lakes, just off Highway 395, it features local rainbow trout, fresh salmon, duck, venison, rack of lamb and many other dishes priced in the $20-30 range. They have a good wine list as well. The second is a steak/prime rib/fresh fish restaurant in Mammoth Lakes, The Mogul (760) 934-3039; http:// TheMogul.com, or e-mail them at Carey@TheMogul.com. They have been in business for over 30 years, a good sign of good food and good service.*

Hike 1—Onion Valley via Kearsarge Pass Trail to the PCT and back

PCT: Access Only
Hike: 12.4 miles
Map: H-1 (Inyo NF)
Difficulty: Difficult
Direction: E→W (RT)

🥾 **Hike.** From the Onion Valley TH, hike W 1.4 miles on the Kearsarge Pass Trail to Gilbert Lake, then another 2.5 miles to Kearsarge Pass. Go W 2.3 miles past Bullfrog Lake to the PCT (10710). From here, you can wander (1) north 2.3 miles to Glen Pass (11978), (2) south on the PCT to Vidette Meadows, or (3) west 0.8 mile down the Charlotte Lake Trail to charming Charlotte Lake (10370). Return by the same route to the Onion Valley TH.

🚗 **Onion Valley CG.** From Independence on Highway 395, go W 12.7 miles on Independence Creek Road 13S17 to the Onion Valley CG and TH.

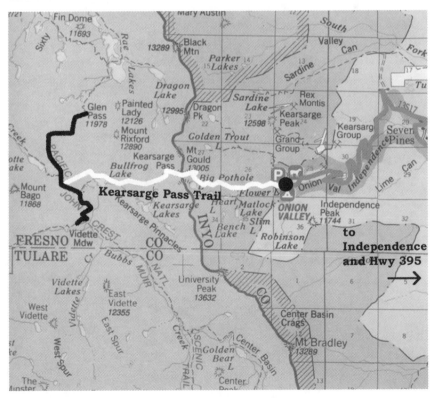

H-1

Hike 2 (Mammoth Lakes Area)—Duck Pass TH in Coldwater CG to Rainbow Falls TH

PCT: 11.3 miles
Hike: 16.5 miles
Map: H-2 (Inyo NF)
Difficulty: Difficult

🏃 **Hike.** Finally, a day hike along the PCT appears! From the Duck Pass TH in the Coldwater CG, hike 5.2 miles up the Duck Pass Trail, past Duck Lake, to the PCT (10150). Go N 7.5 miles on the PCT to Upper Crater Meadows (8920). It is another 3.8 miles down the PCT to a junction (7600) with a broad stagecoach road (the popular Rainbow Falls Trail, a more-than-worthwhile side trip) that leads a short 0.2 mile to the Rainbow Falls TH near the entrance to Reds Meadow Resort and Pack Station.

🚐 **Duck Pass TH in Coldwater CG.** From Highway 395 east of the city of Mammoth Lakes, go W 3.8 miles on Highway 203 to the second traffic signal. Continue straight (W) 3.5 miles on Lake Mary road to Lake Mary Loop road. Turn left (SE)—follow the signs for Lake Mary Marina—and go 0.6 mile to the entrance of the Coldwater CG. Turn left (SE) and go 0.7 mile through the CG to the Duck Pass TH.

🚐 **Rainbow Falls TH near Reds Meadows Resort and Pack Station.** From Highway 395 east of the city of Mammoth Lakes, go W 3.8 miles on

Rainbow Falls

see map H-3

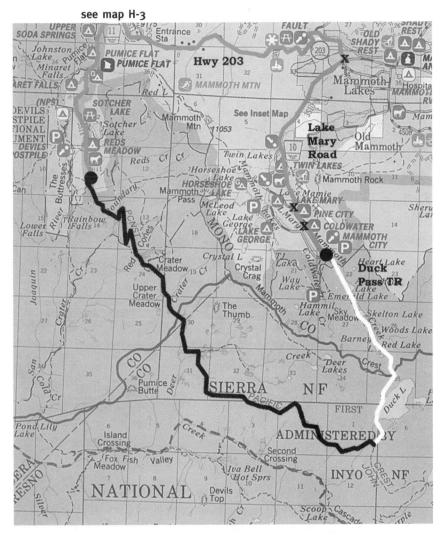

H-2

Highway 203 to the second traffic signal. Turn right (N) on Minaret Road (Highway 203) and go 4.0 miles to Mammoth Ski Area and the first of two USFS kiosks. This kiosk provides information, the most important of which relates to the shuttle-bus system that runs down into valley below.

Continue 1.4 miles to the second USFS kiosk, which is open 7:30-5:25 during the summer to control vehicle traffic into the valley. If you have a camping permit for the valley, you can drive down. If not, you must use the shuttle-bus service operated by Mammoth Ski Resort ($9 round-trip; $5 one-way). If you are not camping in the valley, you can still drive your vehicle into it as long as you do so before 7:30 AM or after 5:25 PM.

From the second USFS kiosk, continue down 2.6 miles to the entrance road to the Agnew Meadows CG—FR 3S55. It is another 5.4 miles to the Rainbow Falls TH near the entrance to Red Meadows Resort and Pack Station.

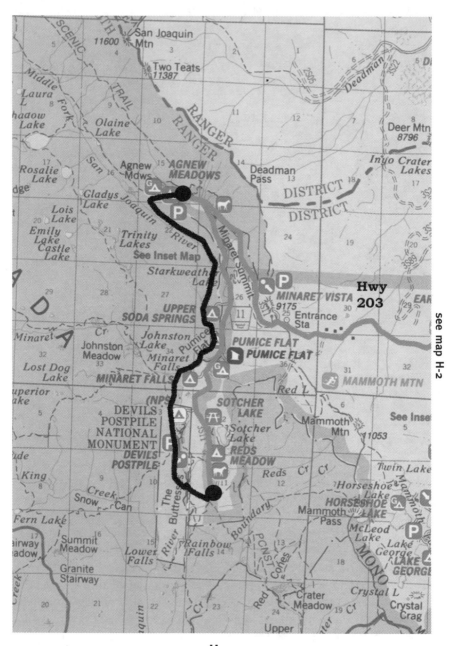

H-3

Hike 3 (Mammoth Lakes Area)—Rainbow Falls TH to Agnew Meadows TH

PCT: 7.8 miles
Hike: 8.0 miles
Map: H-3 (Inyo NF)
Difficulty: Easy

🚶 **Hike.** From the Rainbow Falls TH, hike S 0.2 mile to a junction with the PCT (7600). Go NW 0.5 mile to a trail junction (7430) at the boundary to Devils Postpile National Monument. Continue N 1.6 miles to where the PCT and the John Muir Trail separate (7660). In 0.6 mile, just below awesome Minaret Falls, you cross several branches (7590) of Minaret Creek. (These branches may be deep in early season.) Continue N 1.4 miles to a bridge (7680) over the Middle Fork San Joaquin River. In the next 2.3 miles, cross two streams before reaching a junction (8000) with a trail that parallels the river. In another 0.5 mile, you reach the River Trail (8280), and 0.9 mile further, you reach Agnew Meadows road (8360).

🚐 **Agnew Meadows TH.** From the Rainbow Falls TH, retrace your route 5.4 miles to the entrance road (3S55) to the Agnew Meadows CG. Follow this road 0.3 mile to the TH parking area. (From the second kiosk on Highway 203, it is 2.6 miles down to the Agnew Meadows CG entrance road—FR 3S55.)

Hike 4 (Mammoth Lakes Area)—Agnew Meadows TH to Rush Creek TH near Silver Lake

PCT: 11.0 miles
Hike: 20.4 miles
Map: H-4 (Inyo NF)
Difficulty: Difficult

🚶 **Hike.** From the Agnew Meadows CG (8360), climb N on the PCT to the ridge across from the Ritter Range. In 5.2 miles you intersect a trail (9710) that climbs over Agnew Pass toward Clark Lakes. It is another 2.6 miles on the PCT to Thousand Island Lake (9840), and then another 3.2 miles to the Rush Creek Trail (9600).

Follow the Rush Creek Trail E 2.5 miles past Waugh Lake to a trail junction. Continue on the Rush Creek Trail 1.5 miles to another junction, then another 0.8 mile to where the Alger Lakes Trail departs to the north near the outlet of Gem Lake. Go E 2.5 miles on Rush Creek Trail around Gem Lake to the northeast end of Agnew Lake. It is another 2.1 miles down to the Rush Creek TH near Silver Lake.

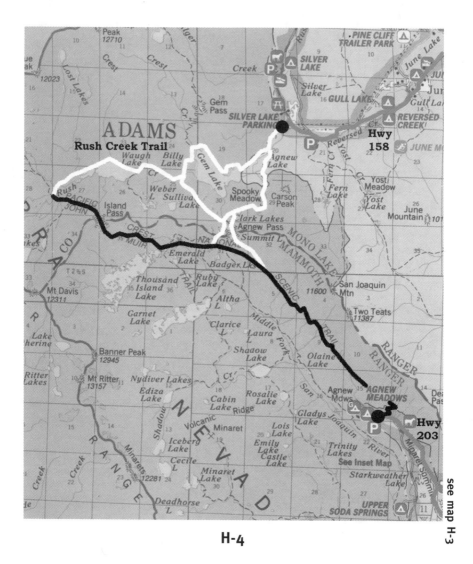

H-4

Several other options. There are several shorter hikes that begin at the Agnew Meadows TH and end at the Rush Creek TH near Silver Lake (7223). The first option covers only 5.2 miles of the PCT as you climb N to the ridge across from the Ritter Range and eventually to a trail (9710) that leads 1.4 miles over Agnew Pass to a trail junction near Clark Lakes.

The second option takes you 0.8 mile further on the PCT to the Middle Fork-Clark Lakes Trail (9500), which makes a steep 1.1 mile ascent over Agnew Pass, then a descent down to Clark Lakes. This is a tough trail, one we would avoid given the other options.

View from ridge above Agnew Meadow

A third option, one we also recommend, takes you 0.3 mile yet further on the PCT to a trail (9590) that leads to Badger Lake, then another 0.2 mile to the third and final trail which you follow 1.1 miles to Clark Lakes.

From Clark Lakes, there are two ways down to the Rush Creek TH. The first, one that may be risky in early season, goes NE 2.5 miles through Spooky Meadow. It intersects the Rush Creek Trail at the northeast end of Agnew Lake. From Agnew Lake, it is 2.1 miles down to the Rush Creek TH near Silver Lake.

The second way down from Clark Lakes is longer, but safer, particularly in early season when snow is still a factor. From the trail junction near Clark Lakes, go NW 2.1 miles to the Rush Creek Trail. Go E 1.5 miles on it to another trail junction. Continue another 0.8 mile on the Rush Creek Trail to where the Alger Lake Trail departs to the north near the outlet to Gem Lake. Go E 2.5 miles on the Rush Creek Trail around Gem Lake to the northeast end of Agnew Lake. It is another 2.1 miles down to the Rush Creek TH near Silver Lake.

🚐 **Rush Creek TH near Silver Lake**. From the Agnew Meadows TH, retrace your route to Highway 395 east of Mammoth Lakes. Turn left (N) on Highway 395 and go 14.5 miles to Highway 158. Turn left (S) on Highway 158 and go 7.1 miles to the Rush Creek TH near Silver Lake. There is ample parking here, not to mention a USFS kiosk, and an illustrated map. (Don't use the map for planning trips, as it contains several errors.)

Hike 5 (Yosemite National Park)—Highway 120 at Tuolumne
Meadows to Rafferty Creek Trail

PCT: 6.9 miles
Hike: 13.8
Map: H-5 (Inyo NF)
Difficulty: Moderate
Direction: N→S (RT)

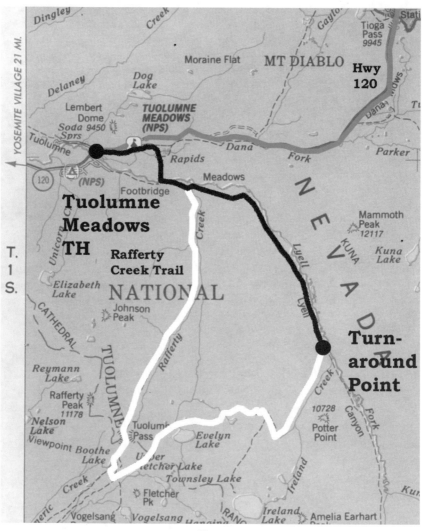

H-5

🚶 **Hike**. The PCT crosses Highway 120 (8595) near Soda Springs road. If you start there, you can park north of Highway 120 on Soda Springs road. Go E 1.1 miles on the PCT to an access trail. This access trail leads to a PCT/John Muir Trail TH parking lot just off Highway 120, where many people will start this hike. Just past the junction of the access trail and the PCT, there is a footbridge (8690) over the Dana Fork of the Tuolumne River. From the footbridge, go S 0.7 mile to a bridge over the Lyell Fork and a trail (8650) that leads west to the Tuolumne Meadows CG. Continue SE on the PCT 0.7 mile to the Rafferty Creek Trail (8710), a trail you might use to end this hike later in the day. For now, continue SE 4.4 miles on the PCT to another trail (8880) that leads to the Vogelsang High Sierra Camp. From this point, you could retrace your steps to Highway 120, or you could follow the trail to the Vogelsang High Sierra Camp, then return via the Rafferty Creek Trail to the PCT 0.7 mile west of the Lyell Fork bridge.

🚗 **Highway 120 at Tuolumne Meadows**. From the junction of Highways 395/120 just south of the town of Lee Vining, go W 12.1 miles on Highway 120 to the Yosemite Park entrance. Continue 6.6 miles to the signed entrance road to the PCT/John Muir Trail TH parking area. It is another 0.4 mile to Soda Springs road, where the PCT crosses Highway 120.

Access Points from the West

Hike 6 (Mono Hot Springs Area)—Florence Lake to Muir Ranch

PCT: 3.0 miles (Approximate: depends how far you want to go)
Hike: 14.0 miles (Approximate: depends how far you want to go)
Map: H-6 (Sierra NF)
Difficulty: Moderate
Direction: Either (RT)

🚶 **Hike**. There are two ways to do this hike. One involves hiking along the Florence Lake Trail 3.2 miles to the spur trail to the ferry landing at the east end of the lake and going on from there. The other is to take the ferry from Florence Lake Resort to the ferry landing and then the spur trail to the main trail. We make the ferry assumption in calculating mileage for this hike.

We recommend that you reserve a ferry time with the Florence Lake Resort in advance. The earlier you leave, the better. Also, we strongly suggest that if you plan to take the ferry back, you plan your day hike

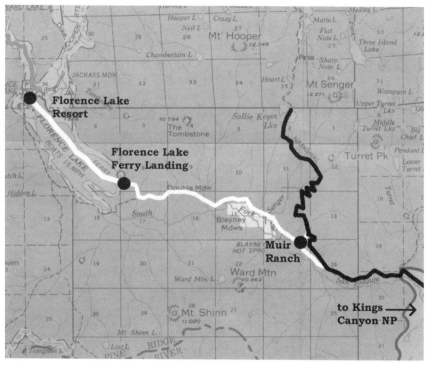

H-6

carefully. If, for some reason, you do not reach the ferry landing in time for the last ferry of the day, you are up a lake without a paddle so-to-speak, and doomed to a 3.2-mile hike back to the Florence Lake TH.

From the ferry landing, it is 0.4 mile to the Florence Lake Trail. Go E 3.0 miles on the Florence Lake Trail to Muir Trail Ranch, where you have two options. First, you can take the cut-off trail NE 0.6 mile to the PCT (8400). From here, it is 3.7 miles north to Selden Pass. Second, you can go SE 1.5 miles to the PCT (7890), then SE another 1.8 miles to the Piute Pass Trail. Whether you go north or south on the PCT, the views in either direction are spectacular. Just remember that if you have a ferry reserved for the trip back to Florence Lake Resort, watch your time carefully.

Yet another option is to stay at the Muir Trail Ranch (www.muirtrail-ranch.com), from which you can do longer hikes north and/or south on the PCT.

🚐 **Florence Lake Resort and Florence Lake TH**. From Fresno, go NE about 50 miles on Highway 168 to the general store in Pine Ridge. Continue E 26.0 miles on Highway 168 to FR 80. Turn right (NE) and go 5.7 miles to where the road narrows from two lanes to a single lane. This is a narrow road with steep drop-offs and few pull-outs, so go slow and exercise caution, especially when rounding corners. Continue 10.1 miles past Kaiser Pass and FR 5 to the High Sierra Ranger Station. Continue straight (E) 0.9 mile to the junction of Florence Lake and Lake Edison roads. Continue straight (SE) 6.0 miles on Florence Lake road to the Florence Lake TH and Florence Lake Resort, where you can catch the ferry.

Hike 7 (Mono Hot Springs Area)—Vermilion Resort to the 4WD Bear Creek Diversion Dam Road

PCT: 8.6 miles
Hike: 19.5 miles
Map: H-7 (Sierra NF)
Difficulty: Difficult
Direction: N→S (Access)

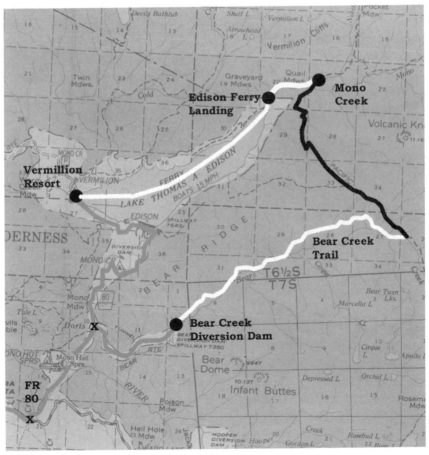

H-7

🚶 **Hike.** To reach the PCT, take the Lake Edison Ferry from Vermilion Resort to the ferry landing at the northeast end of the lake. From here, hike E 1.3 miles to the PCT at North Fork Mono Creek. Turning south on the PCT, you immediately cross North Fork Mono Creek, which can be risky in early season. Go S 0.4 mile to a bridge over Mono Creek (7850), then continue S 4.6 miles to the Bear Ridge Trail (9980). There is a lot of elevation gain along this part of the PCT, over 2000 feet and some 53 switchbacks to be exact. However, because we think it is better to begin the day with the ferry than to miss it at the end of the day, up early in this case is preferred. From the Bear Ridge Trail, continue S 3.6 miles to the Bear Creek Trail (9040), which you follow 7.3 miles down to the Bear Creek Diversion Dam. From here, it is 2.3 miles along a jeep road to Lake Edison road.

🚙 **4WD Bear Creek Diversion Dam Road.** Follow the directions to Florence Lake above (Hike 6) to the High Sierra Ranger Station. Continue straight (E) 0.9 mile to the junction of Florence Lake and Lake Edison roads. Turn left (NE) on Lake Edison road and go 1.7 miles to a crossing of the San Joaquin River and the entrance to Mono Hot Springs. Continue 1.0 mile to the 4WD road that goes to the Bear Creek Diversion Dam.

🚙 **Vermilion Resort.** From the 4WD road that goes to the Bear Creek Diversion Dam, continue NE 2.5 miles on Lake Edison road, past the Mono Creek CG and in front of the dam, to the Vermilion Resort.

A Trans-Sierra Day Hike Experience

For those who want a day hike across the High Sierra, from one side to the other, with parts of the PCT along the way, we have a long hike for you. The logistics are daunting, as you need to arrange for starting and ending points that are a few hundred miles apart across the Sierra divide. Nevertheless, this is an awesome challenge for the dedicated day hiker.

Hike 8 (Mono Hot Springs/Mammoth Lakes Areas)
—Vermilion Resort to Duck Pass TH in Coldwater CG

PCT: 17.7 miles
Hike: 24.2 miles
Maps: H-7, H-8 (Sierra NF), H-2 (Inyo NF)
Difficulty: Difficult

🚶 **Hike.** To reach the PCT, take the Lake Edison Ferry from Vermilion Resort to the ferry landing at the northeast end of the lake. From here, hike

see map H-2

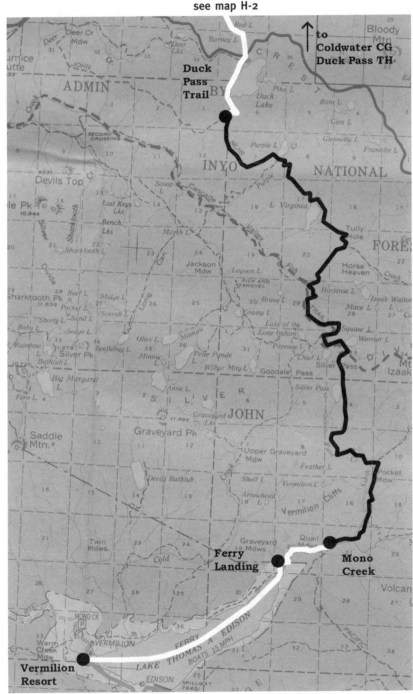

E 1.3 miles to the PCT at North Fork Mono Creek. Turning north on the PCT, you go 1.2 miles to the Mono Pass Trail (8270). In the next 5.4 miles, you cross North Fork Mono Creek near Pocket Meadow (be careful!) and pass to the east of Silver Lake on your way to Silver Pass (10900). Next, you descend N 3.7 miles past the Goodale Pass Trail to the Cascade Valley Trail (9130). Now, go NE 1.1 miles along Fish Creek, crossing it once over a steel bridge, to Tully Hole (9520) and the McGee Pass Trail. Climb steeply N 1.9 miles to Virginia Lake (10314), then down 2.1 miles to Purple Lake (9900). Continue around another high peak 2.3 miles to the Duck Pass Trail (10150) near Duck Lake. Follow the Duck Pass Trail down 5.2 miles to the Duck Pass TH in the Coldwater CG.

While this is a long hike at high altitudes, it provides dedicated day hikers with a way to "bag" another 17.7 miles of the PCT.

Directions to the Duck Lake TH in Coldwater CG are described in Hike H-2 and directions to Vermilion Resort are described in Hike H-7 of Section H.

Tuolumne Meadows to Sonora Pass

Overview

PCT: 14.1 miles
Hikes (3): 24.7 miles
PCT Inaccessible to Day Hikes: 62.3 miles
Declination: 15° E

Section I in the High Sierra is also virtually inaccessible to day hikers. However, we describe two day hikes. One is a round-trip hike in Yosemite National Park, and the other is a challenging (very risky in early season) day hike near Sonora Pass.

Hike 1—Highway 120 at Tuolumne Meadows to Glen Aulin

PCT: 6.0 miles
Hike: 12.0 miles
Map: I-1 (Yosemite National Park)
Difficulty: Moderate
Direction: S→N (RT)

Hike. Proceeding NW 2.0 miles from Highway 120 in Tuolumne Meadows (8595), you cross Delaney Creek before reaching the Young Lakes Trail (8650). In another 2.7 miles, you bridge the Tuolumne River (8310). In a final 1.3 miles you reach Glen Aulin High Sierra Camp (7840), your turn-around point.

Highway 120 at Tuolumne Meadows. From the junction of Highways 395/120 just south of Lee Vining, go W 12.1 miles on Highway 120 to the Yosemite Park entrance. Continue 6.6 miles to the signed entrance to the PCT/John Muir Trail TH parking area. It is another 0.4 mile to Soda Springs road, where the PCT crosses Highway 120.

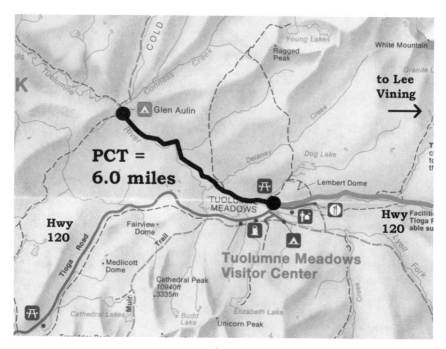

I-1

Tuolumne Meadows

Hike 2—Leavitt Lake road TH to Sonora Pass at Highway 108

PCT: 8.1 miles
Hike: 12.7 miles
Map: I-2 (Stanislaus NF)
Difficulty: Difficult
Direction: N→S (Risk)

Hike. This is a spectacular hike in the High Sierra. However, be careful! Snow may linger long into summer and make portions of this steep hike potentially dangerous. From Highway 108 (8440), follow the jeep road 2.9 miles to Leavitt Lake (9556). From the lake's outlet creek, follow an abandoned jeep road 1.7 miles up to the PCT (10580). From here, the PCT goes NW 3.0 miles around Leavitt Peak to a ridge (10880) above Latopie Lake. The next 0.7 mile of trail traverses a steep wall. Continue

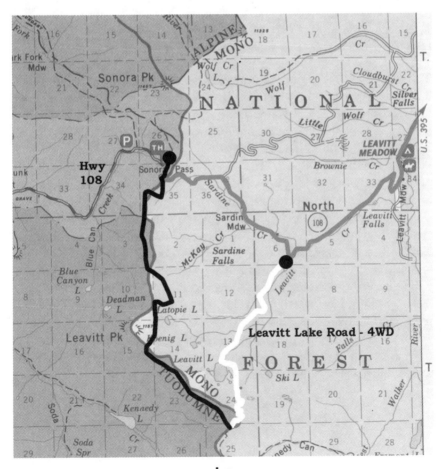

I-2

Distant Tenaya Lake near Tuolumne Meadows

2.0 miles along the ridge to another crossing of the crest (10780). From here, it is down over 1000 feet in 1.7 miles to a series of gullies (9820). The first part of this descent is across very steep slopes, which if snow-covered can be lethal if you fall. Continue down 0.7 mile to Highway 108 at Sonora Pass (9620).

Leavitt Lake Road TH. From the junction of Highway 395/108 north of Bridgeport and south of Walker, go W 11.0 miles on Highway 108 to unsigned Leavitt Lake road. Turn left (S). You will know you are on the right road when in 0.2 mile you encounter a gate and are greeted with a sign stating that access is restricted. This road is usually closed, but the USFS office in Bridgeport reports that they open it in mid-July. Do not attempt to drive up this road unless you have a high-clearance 4WD! Even then, you are in for some serious 4WD.

Sonora Pass at Highway 108. From the junction of Leavitt Lake road and Highway 108, go W 3.7 miles on Highway 108 to Sonora Pass. There is a TH parking area 0.2 mile west of the pass. (Sonora Pass is 14.7 miles west of the junction of Highways 395/108.) The PCT crosses through this TH.

Sonora Pass to Echo Lake Resort

Overview

PCT: 76.2 miles
Hikes (7): 91.0 miles
Declination: 15.25° E

Within Section J are several access points to the PCT, restoring the possibility of Sierra day hikes. A 4-5 day excursion in Section J involves Hikes 3-7, all of which can be staged from the town of Markleeville. Again, there are short hikes (4.2-8.9 miles) and longer, more rigorous ones (15.8-17.7 miles). We recommend the short hikes first, to acclimate yourself to both elevation and exertion.

Lodging tips in Markleeville. The Alpine Inn (530) 694-2591 rents one bed for $40; two for $50. For a real treat, try M's Bed, Bike, & Bagel (530) 694-9337, a two-room apartment ($125 during the week; $135 on the weekends; continental breakfast included). It is ideal for four people, but can accommodate six. There are several nice amenities (stove, microwave, coffee maker) plus a great deck overlooking Hot Springs Creek.

Hike 1—Sonora Pass at Highway 108 to Clark Fork TH

PCT: 12.4 miles
Hike: 18.1 miles
Map: J-1 (Stanislaus NF)
Difficulty: Difficult
Direction: S→N (Elevation)

🚶 **Hike.** The PCT is hard to follow north of Sonora Pass whether snow is still present or not. Pay careful attention to your map. From the pass (9620), go north through the TH parking area, then 1.9 miles through a series of ascending gullies to a switchback (10080). Continue up 1.0 mile to a saddle (10500). Next, you encounter more steep slopes as you work your way N 1.2 miles to a trail junction (10250) above Wolf Creek Lake.

Here, you begin a healthy descent into East Fork Carson River Canyon, which you follow for 5.2 miles to a flat area (8100) along the river. It is another 3.1 miles to the trail (8590) to Boulder Lake, where you leave the PCT and hike 1.5 miles down to the lake, then follow Boulder Creek another 1.5 miles to the Clark Fork Trail, which you follow west 2.7 miles to the Clark Fork TH.

see map J-2

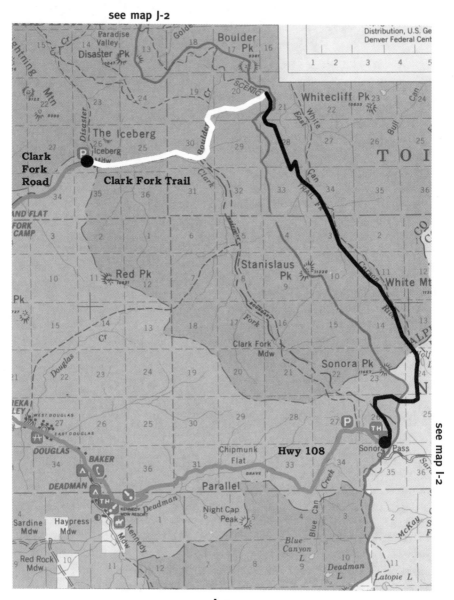

see map I-2

J-1

🚙 **Sonora Pass**. From the junction of Leavitt Lake road and Highway 108 (see the last hike in Section I), go W 3.7 miles on Highway 108 to Sonora Pass. There is a TH parking area 0.2 mile W of the pass. (Sonora Pass is 14.7 miles west of the junction of Highways 395/108.) The PCT crosses through this TH.

🚙 **Clark Fork TH**. From Sonora Pass, go W 16.7 miles on Highway 108 to Clark Fork Road. Turn right (NE) and follow this paved road 9.0 miles to the TH parking area.

Kinney reservoir near Ebbetts Peak

Hike 2—Clark Fork TH to Gardner Meadow TH near Highland Lakes

PCT: 12.0 miles
Hike: 19.4 miles
Map: J-2 (Stanislaus NF)
Difficulty: Difficult

🚶 **Hike**. You begin by going E 2.7 miles up the Clark Fork Trail to the Boulder Creek Trail, which you follow 1.5 miles to Boulder Lake. From Boulder Lake it is another 1.5 miles up to the PCT (8590). Go NW on the PCT 1.6 miles to a crossing of Boulder Creek (8600). From here, you climb 2.3 miles to a saddle (9170) near Golden Lake. It is another 1.2 miles to the Paradise Valley Trail (9170)—see the "Alternate Hike" below. From this junction, go 4.2 miles to the east fork of Wolf Creek (8320). In the next 0.9

mile, you cross the middle and west forks. The final 1.8 miles take you to Wolf Creek Pass (8410), where you depart the PCT and go 1.7 miles down to the Gardner Meadow TH near Highland Lakes.

Alternate Hike (6.9 PCT miles; 14.6 day hike miles). An alternate way to reach the PCT, which reduces your walk on it by 5.1 miles, is to start at the Disaster Creek TH, just 100 yards back down Clark Fork road from its end. Go N 2.7 miles on the Disaster Creek Trail to Adams Camp. Continue NE on the Disaster Creek Trail through Paradise Valley 3.3 miles to the PCT (9170). From here, it is 6.9 miles on the PCT (see the

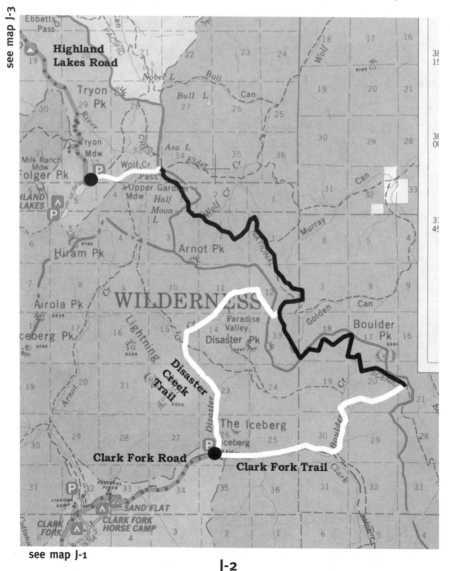

see map J-3

see map J-1

J-2

above hike for details) to Wolf Creek Pass (8410), from where you descend 1.7 miles to the Gardner Meadow TH near Highland Lakes.

🚐 **Gardner Meadow TH near Highland Lakes.** From the Clark Fork TH, retrace your route over Sonora Pass to the junction of Highways 395/108. Turn left (N) on Highway 395 and go 23.1 miles to Highway 89. Turn left (W) and go 17.5 miles to Highway 4. Turn left (SW) and go 13.0 miles to Ebbetts Pass. (Ebbetts Pass is where Hike 3 ends.) Continue W 1.4 miles on Highway 4 to Highland Lakes Road. Turn left (S) on this dirt road and go 4.9 miles to the Gardner Meadow TH.

Hike 3—Gardner Meadow TH near Highland Lakes to Ebbetts Pass

PCT: 7.2 miles
Hike: 8.9 miles
Map: J-3 (Stanislaus NF)
Difficulty: Moderate

🥾 **Hike.** From the Gardner Meadow TH near Highland Lakes, hike up 1.7 miles to the PCT at Wolf Creek Pass (8410). Go N 2.8 miles to your first intersection with the Noble Canyon Trail (9110), just before Noble Lake. This thread of the Noble Canyon Trail goes east down Bull Canyon. The PCT continues N 1.5 miles to the northbound thread of the same trail (8360). Continue 2.9 miles to Highway 4 (8700), just 200 yards northeast of Ebbetts Pass.

🚐 **Ebbetts Pass.** From the Gardner Meadow TH near Highland Lakes, return to Highway 4. Turn right (E) on Highway 4 and go 1.4 miles to Ebbetts Pass. A TH parking area is 0.4 mile east of the pass, a short hike from the PCT. The PCT crosses Highway 4 0.1 mile east of the pass.

Hike 4—Ebbetts Pass to Blue Lakes Road

PCT: 17.7 miles
Hike: 17.7 miles
Map: J-4 (Eldorado NF)
Difficulty: Moderate

🥾 **Hike.** From Ebbetts Pass (8700), go W, then N, 4.0 miles to Raymond Meadows Creek (8640). Continue N 3.0 miles to Pennsylvania Creek (8140). In another 2.5 miles, you reach a spur trail (8640) that leads down to Raymond Lake. In another 1.0 mile, you descend to, and ford, Raymond Lake Creek (8150). Winding your way SW, in 3.9 miles you

138

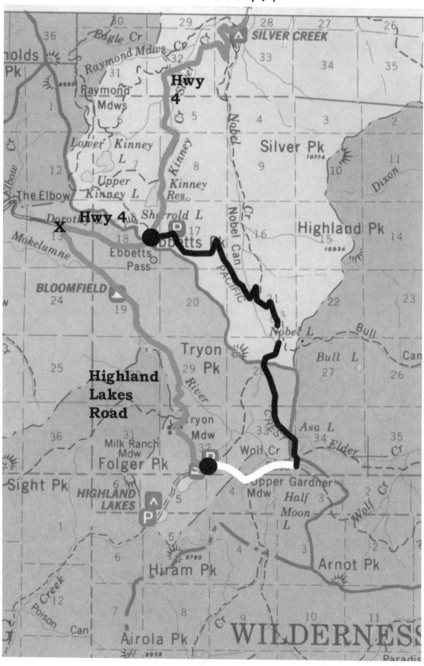

J-3

arrive at Lower Sunset Lake (7900). Continue 3.3 miles to Blue Lakes Road (8090).

🚗 **Blue Lakes Road**. Retrace your route from Ebbetts Pass to the junction of Highways 4/89. Continue straight (N) and go 11.1 miles on Highway 4/89 to the junction of Highways 88/89. (Highway 4 ends here.) Turn left (W) on these concurrent roads and go 5.8 miles to where Highway 89 departs to the north. Bear left (W) on Highway 88 and go 2.4 miles to Blues Lakes Road (FR 15). Turn left (SE) and go 6.9 miles to where the pavement ends. Continue 3.1 miles on dirt Blue Lakes Road to the PCT (8090). This crossing is not well marked. There is limited parking

see map J-5

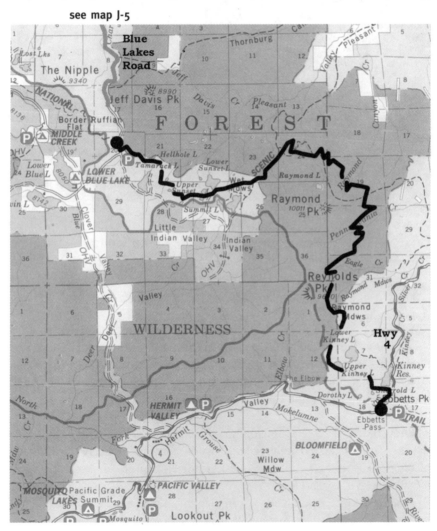

J-4

on either side of this usually dusty road. If you get to the junction of Tamarack Lake and Blue Lakes roads, you've gone 0.4 mile too far. However, do not despair. Turn left (E) on Tamarack Lake Road (FR 097) and go 0.2 mile to a PCT TH parking area.

Charity Creek on Blue Lakes Road; the Nipple in the background

Hike 5—Blue Lakes Road to Lost Lakes Spur Road

PCT: 4.2 miles
Hike: 4.2 miles
Map: J-5 (Eldorado NF)
Difficulty: Easy

Hike. We realize this is a short hike, but we include such hikes for those who might want just a small sample of the PCT. If you camp in the area, this hike, and the next one, can be a nice introduction to the PCT. Of course, you can combine these two hikes into a 11.1-mile hike along the PCT.

From Blue Lakes Road (8090), hike NW 2.4 miles to a saddle (8830) at the southeast base of The Nipple. Now, descend moderately with views of Blue Lakes to the south on your 1.8-mile trek to Lost Lakes spur road (8660) where it meets FR 013 .

Lost Lake Spur Road. From where the PCT crosses Blue Lakes Road (FR 15), continue straight (SW) and go 1.4 miles to Lower Blue Lake. Turn right (NW) and go 3.0 miles along the shores of Lower and Upper Blue lakes to the northwest corner of Upper Blue Lake, where FR 013 turns northeast. At this point, the road becomes rough, perhaps too rough for many passenger cars. Turn right (N) on FR 013 and go 0.8 mile up to where it meets Lost Lake spur road and the PCT. (If NFR 013 is too rough, park near Upper Blue Lake and walk 0.8 mile up FR 013.)

PAT'S TURN TO FALL

If you do this hike in early season, you may encounter steep snow banks that can be difficult to cross. Pat learned this the hard way in July 1999 when she fell down one. No serious injuries, but there could have been. Remember to exercise caution when crossing snow banks, especially steep ones.

see map J-4

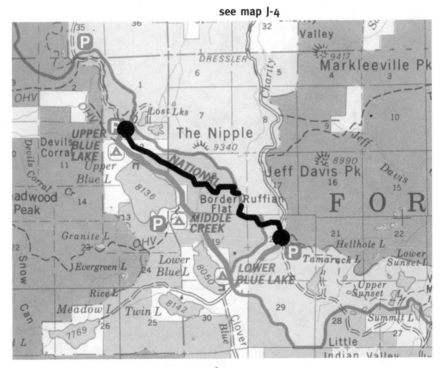

J-5

Hike 6—Lost Lakes Spur to Carson Pass on Highway 88

PCT: 6.9 miles
Hike: 6.9 miles
Map: J-6 (Eldorado NF)
Difficulty: Easy

Hike. From the Lost Lakes spur road (8660), the PCT parallels FR 013 for the first few minutes. In 1.8 miles you intersect Summit City Canyon Trail 18E07 (8880). In the next 4.0 miles, you circle around Elephants Back to the northwest before intersecting trails to Winnemucca Lake and Frog Lake (8870). A short, 1.1-mile descent brings you to Carson Pass (8550) at Highway 88.

Carson Pass. Retrace your route on Blue Lakes Road to Highway 88. Turn left (W) and go 6.2 miles to Carson Pass, where you will find a USFS office and TH parking (fee required).

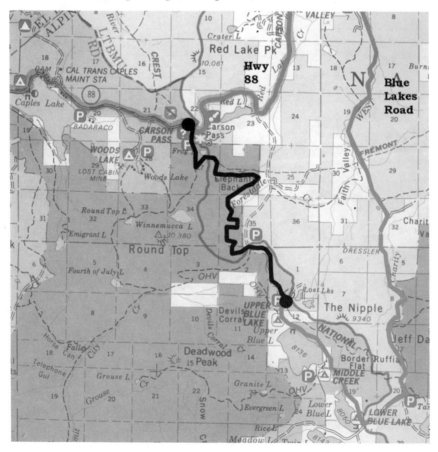

J-6

Pat attempting to cross a snow field near the Nipple

Hike 7—Carson Pass on Highway 88 to Echo Lake Resort

PCT: 15.8 miles
Hike: 15.8 miles
Map: J-7 (Eldorado NF)
Difficulty: Moderate

Hike. From the Carson Pass TH (8550), go NW 3.1 miles to the Meiss Meadow Trail (8380), passing the headwaters of the Upper Truckee River along the way. Continue NW 0.6 mile to a major ford of the Upper Truckee (8310), then 1.6 miles to Showers Lake. In the next 4.4 miles, you intersect Trail 17E16 (8960) and Sayles Canyon Trail 17E14 (8630) before reaching a trail junction in Bryan Meadow (8540). Now descend 2.9 miles through Benwood Meadow to a junction (7475) at the meadow's north edge. Continue N 1.0 mile through Echo Summit Ski area to a TH parking area near the Echo Summit entrance off Highway 50. It is another 2.2 miles along Highway 50 and through a residential area, to Echo Lake Resort on Lower Echo Lake (7414). (Stopping at Echo Summit cuts 2.2 uninteresting miles off this day hike.)

Echo Lake Resort. From Carson Pass, retrace your route 6.2 miles to Highway 88/89. Follow these concurrent roads 2.5 miles to where Highway 89 departs to the north. Turn left (N) on Highway 89 and go 11.0 miles to Highway 50 in Meyers. Turn left (W) and go 5.0 miles to Echo

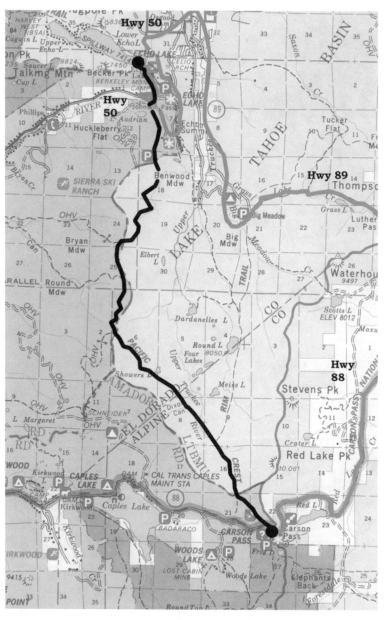

J-7

Lakes road. Turn right (NE) on this road and go 0.5 mile to another Echo
Lakes road sign. Turn left (NW) and go 0.9 mile to the TH parking area.
It is another 0.3 mile down to the resort, Lower Echo Lake, and water-taxi
service. (There is another PCT access point and parking area at Echo
Summit (7390) 0.9 mile east of Echo Lakes road, and 4.1 miles west of the
junction of Highways 89/50 in Meyers.)

Echo Lake Resort to Donner Pass at Interstate 80

Overview

PCT: 63.7 miles
Hikes (5): 78.0 miles
Declination: 15.5° E

All of Section K is in high mountains with glorious vistas along the way. There are several access points to the PCT, making a total of five day hikes possible. The southern part of Section K traverses Desolation Wilderness, the most popular wilderness area in California. The Eagle Falls TH, one access route to this wilderness area and to the PCT near South Lake Tahoe, is the busiest trailhead in all of Tahoe NF. Northbound, you reach Barker Pass (7650), then hike the crest above Alpine Meadows and Squaw Valley ski areas on your way to famous Donner Pass on Old Highway 40 (7090) and finally I-80 near Boreal Ridge (7190).

Hike 1—Echo Lake Resort to Bayview TH or Eagle Falls TH

PCT: 15.0 miles
Hike: 19.2-19.4 miles
Map: K-1 (Eldorado NF)
Difficulty: Moderate

🚶 **Hike.** From the resort on Lower Echo Lake (7414), the PCT parallels the shore NW 3.1 miles to a trail (7700) to Triangle Lake. (An option is to take the Echo Lake water taxi from the resort to the ferry landing at the northwest end of Upper Echo Lake. It is another 0.5 mile from here to the trail to Triangle Lake.) From this junction continue NW 4.4 miles above Tamarack Lake and Lake of the Woods, and along expansive Lake Aloha, to Rubicon River Trail 16E05 (8120), which climbs west to

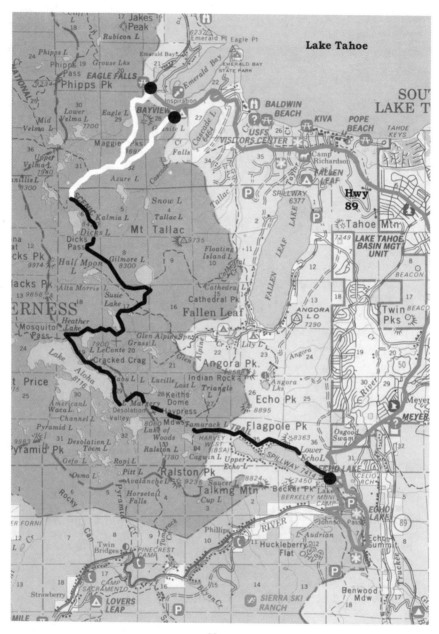

K-1

Mosquito Pass. Turn E and go 1.8 miles to the outlet creek (7790) of Susie Lake, passing Heather Lake. Now, turn NW and begin your climb to Dicks Pass (9380), which you reach in 4.0 miles. Go N 1.7 miles down and around Dicks Lake to a junction with a trail (8500) that leads NE down to the Eagle Falls Trail. Here you depart the PCT and hike 0.9 mile to the

Velma Lakes Trail. Continue NE 0.7 mile on the Velma Lakes Trail to a major junction of the Emerald Bay Trail and the Eagle Falls Trail. Follow the Emerald Bay Trail 2.8 miles down to the Bayview TH, or the Eagle Falls Trail 2.6 miles down to its TH. Of the two trails, Emerald Bay is less popular and more scenic, and has less elevation change.

🚐 **Echo Lake Resort**. From Carson Pass, the starting point of the last hike in Section J, retrace your route 6.2 miles to Highway 88/89. Follow these concurrent roads 2.5 miles to where Highway 89 departs to the north. Turn left (N) on Highway 89 and go 11.0 miles to Highway 50. Turn left (W) and go 5.0 miles to Echo Lakes road. Turn right (NE) and go 0.5 mile to another Echo Lakes road sign. Turn left (NW) and go 0.9 mile to the TH parking area. It is another 0.3 mile down to the resort, Lower Echo Lake, and water-taxi service. (There is another PCT access point and parking area at Echo Summit (7390) 0.9 mile east of Echo Lakes road, and 4.1 miles west of the junction of Highways 89/50.)

🚐 **Bayview TH**. From Echo Lake, retrace your route to the junction of Highways 89/50. Turn left (N) on Highway 89 and go 7.5 miles to Inspiration Point to your right and the Bayview TH CG to your left. Turn left and drive through the CG 0.2 mile to the TH parking area.

🚐 **Eagle Falls TH**. From the Bayview CG TH on Highway 89, go N 0.9 mile to the Eagle Falls TH. There is a $3 daily fee to park at this trailhead, not unreasonable considering just how popular this area is. You can also park across the highway for free, but do not park in undesignated areas—you will get a ticket.

Hike 2—Bayview TH or Eagle Falls TH to FR 3 near Barker Pass

PCT: 17.3 miles
Hike: 21.6 miles
Map: K-2 (Eldorado NF)
Difficulty: Difficult

🚶 **Hike.** From the Bayview TH, hike SW 2.8 miles up to the junction of the Emerald Bay/Eagle Falls/Velma Lakes trails. From the Eagle Falls TH, go SW 2.6 miles up to the same trail junction. (Of the two trails, Emerald Bay is less popular but more scenic, and it involves several hundred feet less climbing.) Go SW 0.7 mile to a trail junction, then go SW 0.9 mile to the PCT (8500) north of Dicks Lake. (Northbound, you can reach the PCT sooner by following the Velma Lakes Trail NW 0.9 mile to the PCT between Upper and Middle Velma lakes (7965); however, this omits 2.1 miles of the PCT.)

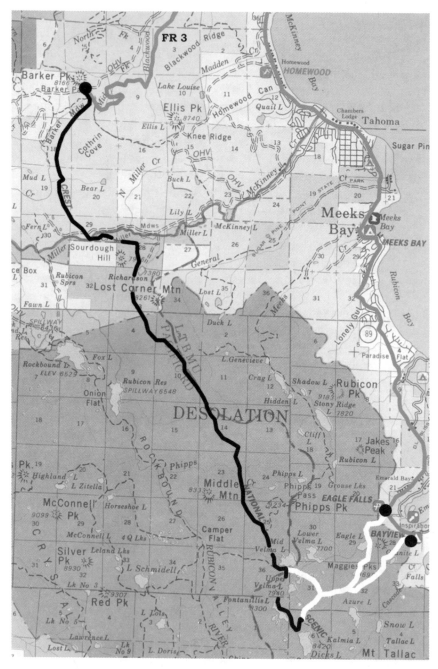

K-2

Once you reach the PCT north of Dicks Lake (8500), go N 2.1 miles to
Middle Velma Lake (7965), where the Velma Lakes Trail departs east. In

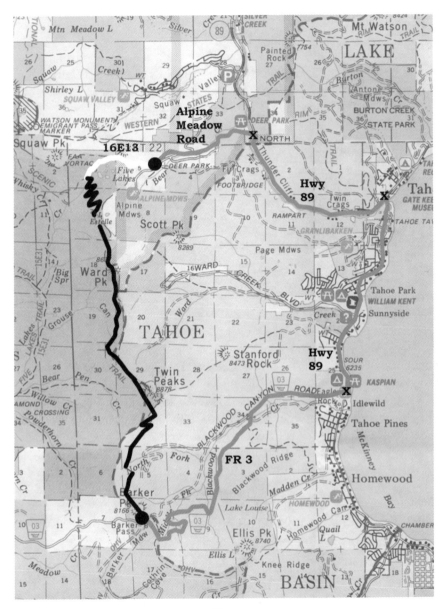

K-3

another 0.3 mile, the Velma Lakes Trail (7940) departs west toward Camper Flat. Continue NW 8.7 miles, past Middle Mountain to the west and Lost Corner Mountain to the east, to the northwest corner of Richardson Lake (7400). It is another 1.9 miles to McKinney-Rubicon Springs road (7000), a rough jeep road that leads E about 8.0 miles to

Highway 89. Continue N 1.9 miles to Bear Lake road (7120), then 2.4 miles to FR 3 near Barker Pass (7650).

🚗 **FR 3 near Barker Pass.** From the Eagle Falls TH, go N 14.3 miles on Highway 89 to Blackwood Canyon road (FR 3). Turn left (W) and go 6.8 miles to the crest, where the pavement ends. Continue 0.5 mile down this good dirt road to the PCT and a TH parking area.

Hike 3—FR 3 near Barker Pass to Alpine Meadows Road

PCT: 11.4 miles
Hike: 13.9 miles
Map: K-3 (Tahoe NF)
Difficulty: Moderate

🥾 **Hike.** From FR 3 (7650) near Barker Pass, wind N 2.4 miles to the headwaters of North Fork Blackwood Creek (7960). In the next 2.4 miles, you climb to a low knoll (8370), then work around Twin Peaks and along the crest 3.5 miles to near Wards Peak (8470). Continue N 3.1 miles, descending at the end via 16 switchbacks to the Five Lakes Trail (7430), where you leave the PCT to go northeast. Go 0.6 mile to Five Lakes, then continue down 1.9 miles on Five Lakes Trail 16E13 to Alpine Meadows road and a small TH parking area.

🚗 **Five Lakes TH on Alpine Meadow Road.** From the junction of Highway 89 and Blackwood Canyon road, go N 7.9 miles on Highway 89 to Alpine Meadows road. Turn left (W) and go 2.1 miles to the Five Lakes TH at Deer Park road. (If you are coming from I-80 to the north in Truckee, go S 9.9 miles on Highway 89 to Alpine Meadows road.)

Hike 4—Alpine Meadows Road to old Highway 40 near Donner Pass

PCT: 17.0 miles
Hike: 19.5 miles
Map: K-4 (Tahoe NF)
Difficulty: Moderate

🥾 **Hike.** From Alpine Meadows road, hike up 1.9 miles on Five Lakes Trail 16E13 to Five Lakes. Continue SW 0.6 mile to the PCT (7430). In the first 3.7 miles on the PCT, you pass Whiskey Creek Trail 16E06 (7170), then meet Tevis Cup Trail 16E09 (7915), which you follow across the headwaters of Middle Fork American River, to where the Tevis Cup Trail departs to the east (8140). The PCT continues N 2.2 miles across the crest and

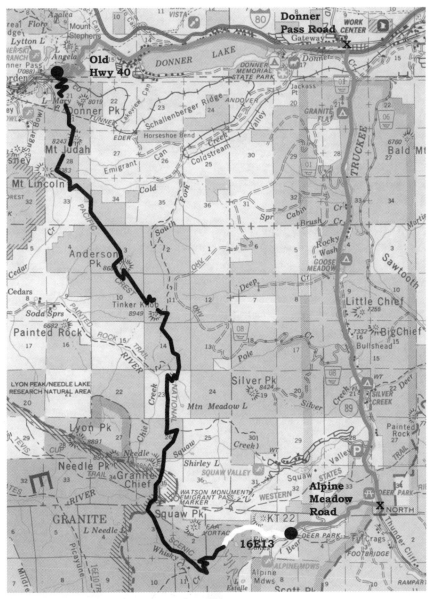

K-4

across the headwaters of Squaw Creek to Granite Chief Trail 15E23 (8170). Continue N 3.7 miles past Painted Rock Trail 15E06 (7550) to Tinker Knob Saddle (8590). In another 5.4 miles you reach Roller Pass (7900). The last 2.0 miles take you to Old Highway 40 near Donner Pass (7090).

Donner Pass on old Highway 40. From Alpine Meadows road, retrace your route to Highway 89. Go N 9.9 miles on Highway 89 and

under Highway I-80 in Truckee to Donner Pass road (old Highway 40).
Turn left (W) on Donner Pass road and go 7.8 miles to the PCT and the
Donner Pass TH parking area.

Hike 5—Old Highway 40 near Donner Pass to Boreal Ridge near I-80

PCT: 3.0 miles
Hike: 3.7 miles
Map: K-5 (Tahoe NF)
Difficulty: Easy

Hike. From Old Highway 40 (7090), the PCT meanders 3.0 miles to
a trail junction (7190) south of the tunnel under Highway I-80, where
Section K ends. Follow the spur trail W 0.7 mile to the PCT TH parking
near the Boreal Ridge exit off I-80.

Boreal Ridge near I-80. From the junction of Highways I-80/89 in
Truckee, go W 8.5 miles on Highway I-80 to the Boreal Ridge exit. Go
south under I-80, then E 0.4 mi. to the PCT TH parking area.

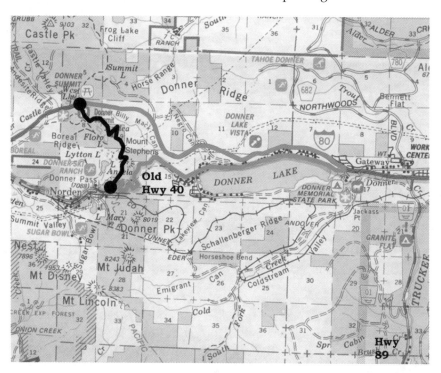

K-5

Donner Pass at Interstate 80 to Highway 49 near Sierra City

Overview

PCT: 38.4 miles
Hikes (3): 39.1 miles
Declination: 15.75° E

The Schaffer guide suggests that this 38.4-mile section can be done as a day hike by strong hikers. That is their definition of a day hike. Our definition of a day hike is significantly less that 38.4 miles. We have tried to keep the hikes to less than 20 miles, something we feel most people in reasonably good condition can do in a day. Some of our hikes are a little longer, but only when it is necessary.

Again, our goal is to appeal to as many people as possible who want to access the PCT in relatively small, manageable chunks. At the same time, we have written this book so that more adventurous folks can combine some hikes into longer endeavors if they desire.

Hike 1—Boreal Ridge near I-80 to Meadow Lake Road 19N11

PCT: 15.9 miles
Hike: 16.6 miles
Map: L-1A and L-1B (Tahoe NF)
Difficulty: Moderate

Hike. From the Boreal Ridge TH, hike E 0.7 mile to the PCT (7190) at the end of Section K and the beginning of Section L. Turn N, go under Highway I-80, then up Castle Valley to Castle Pass (7910), a total of 3.3 miles. It is another 0.9 mile to the Sierra Club's Peter Grubb Hut (7820). Continue N 4.1 miles, past Basin Peak and over North Creek, to Magonigal Camp jeep road (7580). Continue NW 2.3 miles to White Rock

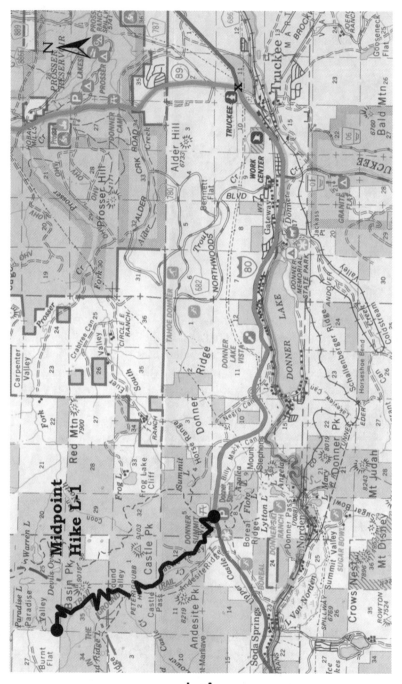

L-1A

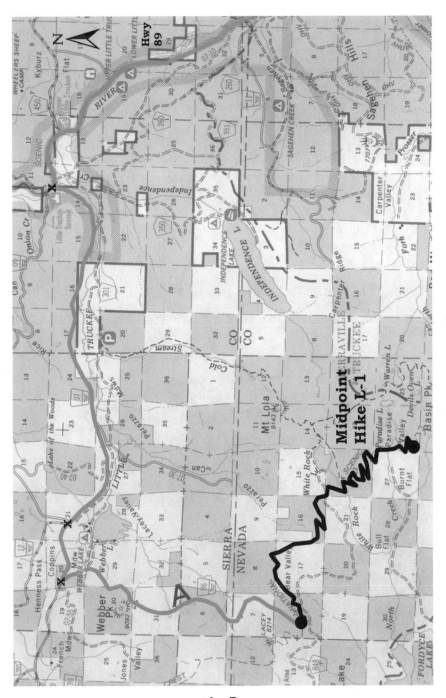

L-1B

Creek (7630). You intersect FR 19N11A (7660) in 0.7 mile, then shortly turn west for a 4.6-mile trek across Bear Valley on your way to Meadow Lake Road 19N11 (7530). (The Schaffer guide calls FR 19N11 Tahoe FR 86 in the text, but shows it as 19N11 on their map. In fact, these refer to the same road as it progresses north from Lacey Creek—see below.)

Boreal Ridge near I-80. From the junction of Highways I-80/89 in Truckee, go W 8.5 miles on Highway I-80 to the Boreal Ridge exit. Go south under I-80, then E 0.4 mile to the PCT TH parking area.

Meadow Lake Road 19N11—also Tahoe FR 86 from Lacey Creek. From Boreal Ridge near I-80, retrace your route on I-80 to the junction of Highways I-80/89 in Truckee. Continue E 2.1 miles on Highway I-80/89 to the Highway 89/267 exit off I-80. Turn left (N) on Highway 89 and go 14.5 miles to FR 7. Turn left (W) on FR 7 and go 8.2 miles to FR 12. (This junction is important in getting to one of the trailheads in Hike 3). Continue W 1.3 miles on FR 7 to FR 86. Turn left (S) on FR 86 and go 5.1

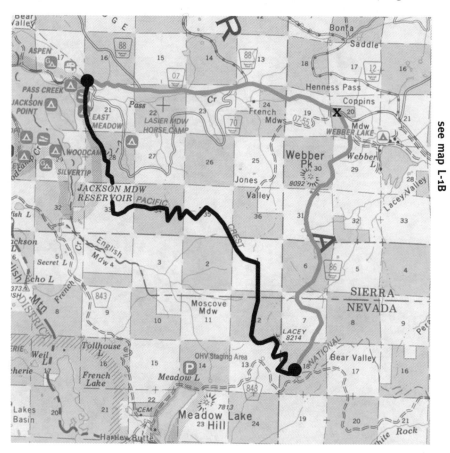

L-2

miles to a signed crossing of Lacey Creek . At this point, FR 86 becomes Meadow Lake Road 19N11. Continue S 1.4 miles up this road to the PCT. If you reach a major road intersection, you have gone 0.2 mile past the PCT.

Hike 2—Meadow Lake Road 19N11 to FR 7 near Jackson Meadow Reservoir

PCT: 11.6 miles
Hike: 11.6 miles
Map: L-2 (Tahoe NF)
Difficulty: Moderate

🚶 **Hike.** From Road 19N11 (7530), head up 1.1 miles to a ridge (8000), then down slightly 2.1 miles to a logging road (7640). Head NW 3.6 miles to a seasonal creek (7330), then cross several roads in the next 4.8 miles as you descend to paved FR 7 (6200) near Jackson Meadow Reservoir.

🚗 **FR 7 near Jackson Meadow Reservoir.** From Meadow Lake Road 19N11, retrace your route on FR 86 to FR 7. (At the junction of FR 86/7, you are 9.5 miles west of Highway 89.) Turn left (W) on FR 7 and go 5.3 miles to the PCT and FR 70. There is no place to park on FR 7. Turn left (S) on FR 70 and go 0.4 mile to Lasier Meadow Horse Camp, and another crossing of the PCT, where you can park. The East Meadow CG is 0.4 mile further south along FR 70.

Hike 3—FR 7 near Jackson Meadow Reservoir to Highway 49 near Sierra City

PCT: 10.9 miles
Hike: 10.9 miles
Map: L-3 (Tahoe NF)
Difficulty: Moderate

🚶 **Hike.** From FR 7 (6200), the first 6.3 miles take you NW up to a ridge, across another Bear Valley, and down along Milton Creek to your first crossing of it (5240). Descending another 0.8 mile, you cross the creek again (4990), this time on a bridge. From here, proceed 1.2 miles to a road (4810). Continue NW 2.6 miles across two more bridges over Haypress Creek (4720) and North Yuba River (4600) on your way to Highway 49 (4570).

🚗 **Highway 49 near Sierra City—several options.**
Paved road; longest option. From Jackson Meadow Reservoir, retrace your route E 14.7 miles on FR 7 to Highway 89. Turn left (N) on Highway

BEARS IN BEAR VALLEY

We knew we were in for an interesting evening when the two young, male occupants of the adjacent campsite returned with four cases of beer. As the evening wore on, their campfire got bigger, and bigger, and bigger, until it reached what any reasonable person would call a bonfire. Shortly before midnight, our neighbors must have passed out because the fire began to subside and no more sounds came from their campsite.

An hour later, things changed. We were awakened by loud screams that were not of human origin. Lured by an open ice chest, a bear was ravaging our neighbor's campsite. At this point, things got interesting. Our macho neighbors started fighting with the bear for the food! Soon everyone, the two males and the bear, were screaming as loud as they could. This lasted for nearly ten minutes until the bear finally turned around and sauntered away. That was one of the most bizarre "interactions" we have seen in our hikes along the PCT.

89 and go 8.8 miles to the junction of Highways 89/49. Bear left (NW) on Highway 49/89 and go 4.9 miles to where Highway 89 departs north and Highway 49 departs west. Turn left (W) on Highway 49 and go 16.3 miles to the small PCT TH parking area east of Sierra City.

Dirt road; shorter option. From Jackson Meadow Reservoir, retrace your route E 6.6 miles on FR 7 to FR 12. Turn left (N) and go 10.4 miles to the junction of FR 12 and FR 54. Stay on FR 12 and go 5.8 miles to Highway 49 at Yuba Pass. Turn left (W) and go 10.2 miles to the small PCT TH parking area east of Sierra City.

Marginal dirt road; shortest option. From Jackson Meadow Reservoir, retrace your route E 6.6 miles on FR 7 to FR 12. Turn left (N) on FR 12 and go 10.4 miles to the junction of FR 12 and FR 54. Follow marginal FR 54 6.0 miles to where this rough dirt road ends and the pavement begins. Continue 6.6 miles on now paved, one-lane FR 54 to Highway 49 at Bassetts Station. Turn left (W) on Highway 49 and go 3.5 miles to the small PCT TH parking area east of Sierra City.

(Sierra City is 1.5 miles southwest of the TH. On your way to Sierra City, you will meet Road 20N13, which you can follow S 2.1 miles to Wild Plum Falls. Here you will find parking, a PCT access trail, and a CG.)

Lodging and dining tips in Sierra City. Herrington's Sierra Pines Lodge and Motel (530) 862-1511 offers nice rooms at reasonable rates ($45-55). They also have a restaurant. It is somewhat pricey, but there are some reasonable values, like the Chicken Caesar salad. If you don't like what's on the menu, you can always pay them to catch a fresh trout from their trout pond. Where do you cook it? The motel has a grill and cooking ring directly across the street for use by all their guests. That's where we cooked breakfast each day, despite the hordes of gnats.

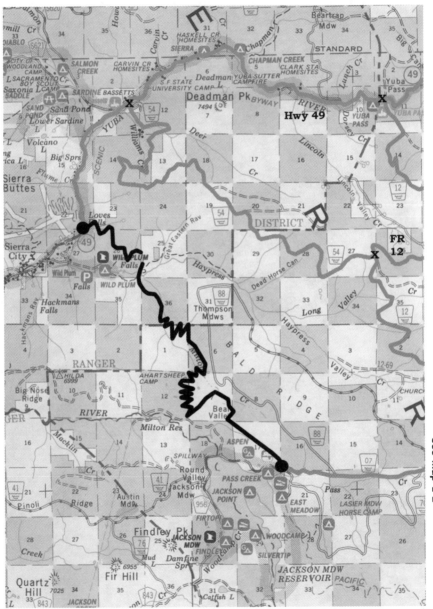

see map L-2

L-3

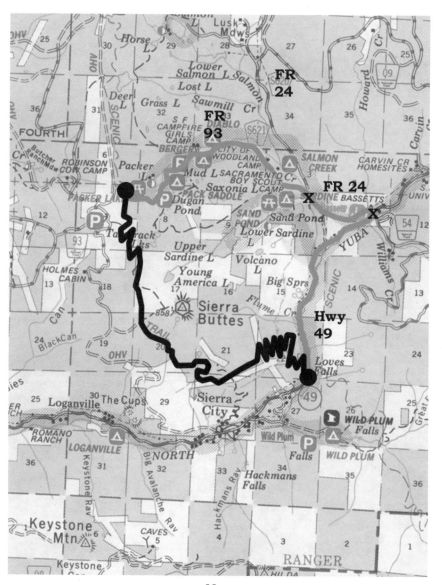

M-1

Highway 49 near Sierra City to Highway 70 near Belden Town Bridge

Overview

PCT: 91.7 miles
Hikes (8): 92.3 miles
Declination: 16° E

Great contrast occurs as you hike from Sierra City (4570) up to a crest (7150) near Sierra Buttes. After staying on the crest for several miles, eventually you descend and pass through a deep canyon created by the Middle Fork Feather River (2900). In the last part of the section, you climb again, to Bucks Summit (5531), traverse Bucks Lake Wilderness, and then descend into the deep canyon created by the East Branch North Fork Feather River (2330).

Hike 1—Highway 49 near Sierra City to Packer Lake Saddle

PCT: 9.8 miles
Hike: 9.8 miles
Map: M-1 (Tahoe NF)
Difficulty: Easy
Direction: N→S (Elevation)

Hike. The PCT begins this section 1.5 miles east of Sierra City on Highway 49 (4570) with an ascent of over 1000 feet as it switches up 2.7 miles to a flume (5720). It then climbs more gradually 4.5 miles to the Sierra Buttes jeep road (7150). You stay on the crest as you work your way north 2.6 miles to Packer Lake Saddle (7020).

Highway 49 near Sierra City. (Please see the end of the last section (L) for several ways to get to Sierra City from FR 7 near Jackson Meadow Reservoir, where the last day hike began.) To reach Sierra City, go to the junction of Highways 49/89. Turn left (W) on Highway 49 and

see map M-3

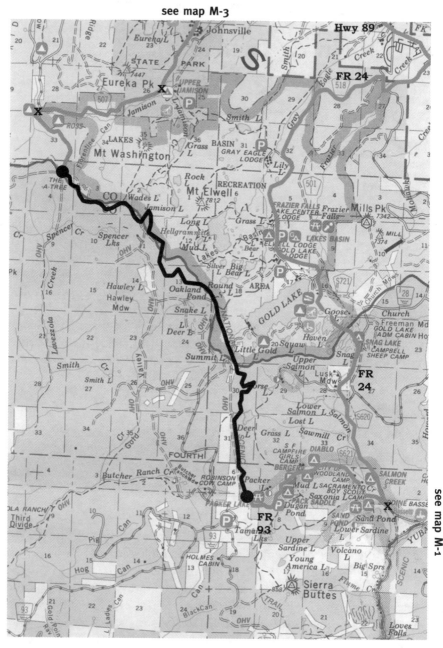

see map M-1

M-2

go 16.3 miles to the small PCT TH parking area east of Sierra City. (Sierra City is 1.5 miles southwest of the TH. On your way to Sierra City, you will meet Road 20N13, which you can follow S 2.1 miles to Wild Plum Falls. Here you will find parking, a PCT access trail, and a CG.)

Packer Lake Saddle. From the PCT TH on Highway 49 east of Sierra City, go E 3.5 miles on Highway 49 to FR 24 at Bassetts Station. Turn left (W) on FR 24 and go 1.3 miles to Packer Lake road. (At the junction of FR 24 and Packer Lake road, you are 14.0 miles south of the junction of FR 24 and Highway 89 in Graeagle.) Turn left (W) on Packer Lake road and go 0.3 mile to a major intersection. Turn right (NW) toward Packer Lake—follow the sign to FR 93—and go 2.6 miles to a sign that says FR 93 BEGIN. Follow FR 93 1.6 miles up to the PCT at Packer Lake Saddle. To park, go S 0.6 mile (this road and the PCT are one and the same) to the Sierra Buttes TH. The last 0.2 mile of this road is unpaved.

Hike 2—Packer Lake Saddle to the A-Tree Saddle

PCT: 12.5 miles
Hike: 12.5 miles
Map: M-2 (Tahoe NF)
Difficulty: Moderate

Hike. Leaving Packer Lake Saddle, you stay on the crest as you go N 4.4 miles to Summit Lake road (7050). Turning northwest, you stay true to the crest for the next 8.1 miles to the A-Tree Saddle (6550).

The A-Tree Saddle. From Packer Lake Saddle, retrace your route to FR 24. Turn left (N) on FR 24 and go 14.0 miles to Highway 89 in Graeagle. Turn left (N) and go 1.4 miles to County Road A14. Turn left (W) and go 5.1 miles—follow the signs for Johnsville Ski Area—to the Eureka State Park Museum. Turn left into the museum parking lot and follow the one-lane, paved CG road SW 1.1 miles to Upper Jamison Creek CG. Go SW 3.4 miles on this rough dirt road to a major, unsigned road junction 0.3 mile past Ross Camp. Turn left (SW) and go 2.1 miles to the A-Tree Saddle, where the PCT and five roads meet.

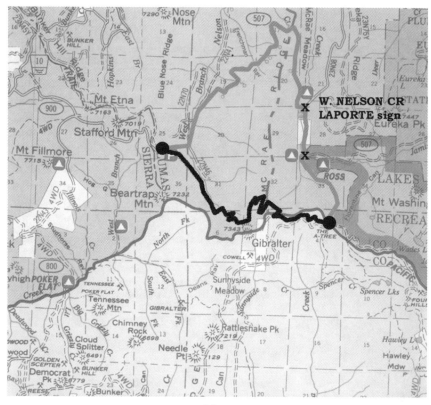

M-3

Hike 3—The A-Tree Saddle to Johnsville-Gibsonville Road

PCT: 7.6 miles
Hike: 7.6 miles
Map: M-3 (Plumas NF)
Difficulty: Easy

Hike. This relatively short hike begins with a modest climb 1.9 miles to a saddle (7380) at the south end of McRae Ridge. From here, you switch down in front of Gibralter's face and in 3.2 miles arrive near the headwaters of West Branch Nelson Creek (6150). You follow the creek down and in 2.5 miles reach Johnsville-Gibsonville road (6065).

Johnsville-Gibsonville Road. From the A-Tree Saddle, retrace your route 2.1 miles to the major, unmarked junction 0.3 mile west of the Ross CG. Turn left (N) and go 1.1 miles to the W. NELSON CR/LA PORTE sign. Follow this rough, unpaved road toward La Porte 7.4 miles to where the PCT crosses it. If you get to a major, exposed ridge, you have gone 0.7 mile too far.

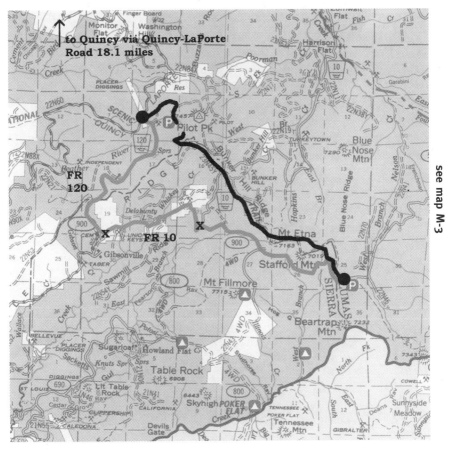

M-4

Hike 4—Johnsville-Gibsonville Road to Quincy-LaPorte Road (FR 120)

PCT: 8.1 miles
Hike: 8.1 miles
Map: M-4 (Plumas NF)
Difficulty: Easy

Hike. Proceeding NW 3.0 miles from the start, you skirt Stafford Mountain and Mt. Etna on your way to Bunker Hill Ridge (6750). Following the crest NW for 5.1 miles, you reach Quincy-LaPorte road (6474).

Quincy-LaPorte Road. From the junction of Johnsville-Gibsonville road and the PCT, go W 4.0 miles on this rough dirt road to FR 10. (If this road is too risky for you, and for some it may be, especially in early season, retrace your route to Graeagle. Turn left (NW) on

Highway 70/89 and go to Quincy-LaPorte road (FR 120) east of Quincy. Turn left (S) and go 18.1 miles to the junction of FR 120, FR 60, and the PCT.) For those who brave the rough dirt road and arrive at FR 10, turn left (W) on unpaved FR 10 and go 3.5 miles to unpaved FR 120. Turn right (N) and go 4.5 miles to where the PCT, FR 120, and FR 60 meet. (At this junction, the Quincy-LaPorte road changes FR designations. To the north, toward Quincy, it is FR 120. To the south, toward Little Grass Valley Reservoir, it is FR 60. This is confusing, but if you study the map carefully, you should have no problem navigating in this region.)

Hike 5—Quincy-La Porte Road (FR 120) to Sawmill Tom Creek Road 23N65Y north of Fowler Lake

PCT: 9.8 miles
Hike: 9.8 miles
Map: M-5 (Plumas NF)
Difficulty: Easy

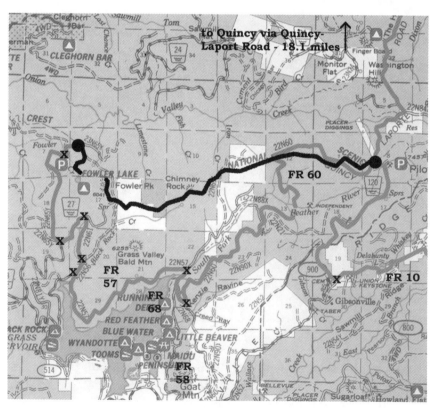

M-5

🚶 **Hike**. Winding your way west and down 4.2 miles, you twice cross FR 60 (Road 22N60) before arriving at the Bear Wallow Trail (5755), a jeep road that leads down a canyon to South Fork Feather River. In the next 1.0 mile, you climb moderately to Chimney Rock (6000), then descend 2.1 miles to Black Rock Creek Road 22N56 (5460). Turn NW for 1.2 miles around Fowler Peak to a trail (5500) that leads down to Fowler Lake. Continue 1.3 miles down to Sawmill Tom Creek Road 23N65Y (5060).

🚗 **Sawmill Tom Creek Road 23N65Y north of Fowler Lake**. From the junction of the PCT, FR 60, and Quincy-La Porte road (FR 120), go W 5.7 miles on FR 60 to where the pavement ends. Continue SW 3.0 miles on FR 60 to FR 68. Turn right (S)—follow the sign for Little Grass Valley Reservoir—and go down 0.9 mile to the junction of FRs 68/57/58 near the northeast corner of the reservoir. Now turn right—follow the sign for Black Rock Creek—and go 4.5 miles on FR 57 around the northeast end of the reservoir to Black Rock Creek road. Turn right (N) and go 0.2 mile to a major, unsigned junction. (There is a PCT marker indicating that you can go either direction to reach the PCT.) Turn left (NW) and go 1.1 mile to the next unsigned junction.

(Here you encounter yet another PCT marker. This one tells you to turn right to get to the PCT. If you turn right, indeed you will reach the PCT in 1.0 mile, where it crosses Black Rock Creek Road 22N56. We chose not to use this access point. Rather we selected Sawmill Tom Creek Road 23N65Y because it makes the next hike (Hike 6), which is very strenuous, 1.3 miles shorter.)

Thus, at this unsigned junction, you will turn left (NW) and go 1.0 mile to the next junction. Here you may be able to see a FR road sign. Make a hard right and go W 2.6 miles to the unsigned junction of Dogwood road and FR 23N65Y. Turn right (N) on 23N65Y and go 0.7 mile to the PCT. (There is a dirt road with rock markers shortly before you reach the PCT. You will know when you reach the real thing because there are PCT markers on both sides of the road.)

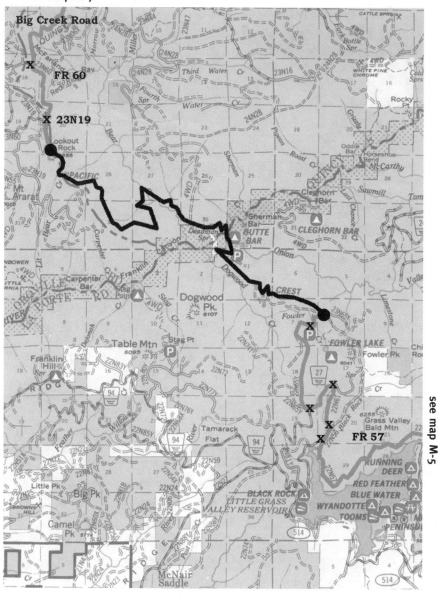

M-6

Hike 6—Sawmill Tom Creek Road 23N65Y north of Fowler Lake to Lookout Rock

PCT: 16.4 miles
Hike: 16.7 miles
Map: M-6 (Plumas NF)
Difficulty: Difficult

🚶 **Hike.** On this hike you first descend 6.1 miles from Sawmill Tom Creek road (5060) into Middle Fork Feather River Canyon, where you cross the river via a huge bridge (2900). From here, the path goes up the other side of the canyon. After 3.5 miles, you cross Bear Creek (3240), then make a long but graded 6.8-mile ascent to Lookout Rock (5955). It is a short 0.3 mile from the PCT to the TH parking area.

🚗 **Lookout Rock.** Retrace your route to the intersection of the PCT, FR 60, and Quincy-La Porte road (FR 120) described at the end of Hike 4. Go N 18.1 miles on FR 120 to Highway 89/70 east of Quincy. Turn left (W) and go 3.6 miles through the town of Quincy to Bucks Lake/Meadow Valley road (FR 119). Turn right (W) on FR 119 and go 9.0 miles through Meadow Valley to the junction of Bucks Lake road and Big Creek road. (At this intersection, Big Creek road is designated as FR 119 on the USFS map.) Bear left (S) on Big Creek road (FR 119) and go 6.5 miles to the Lookout Rock sign and FR 60. Turn left (S) on FR 60 and go 1.7 miles to FR 23N19. Bear left (S) on 23N19 and go 0.5 mile to the Lookout Rock TH. The PCT is 0.3 mile from the TH.

Hike 7—Lookout Rock to Bucks Summit

PCT: 8.4 miles
Hike: 8.7 miles
Map: M-7 (Plumas NF)
Difficulty: Easy

🚶 **Hike.** From the TH parking area, hike 0.3 mile to the PCT. Back on the crest near Lookout Rock (5955), you proceed NW 3.6 miles across FR 23N19 and above Bucks Lake to a crossing of FR 33N56 (5505). Continuing north you parallel Big Creek road 4.8 miles to Bucks Summit (5531) at Bucks Lake road.

🚗 **Bucks Summit.** Retrace your route from Lookout Rock to the junction of Bucks Lake road and Big Creek road. (You are now 9.0 miles west of Highway 70/89 in Quincy.) Make a hard left (SW)—bear right if you are coming from Quincy—and go up 3.2 miles on Bucks Lake road to the summit.

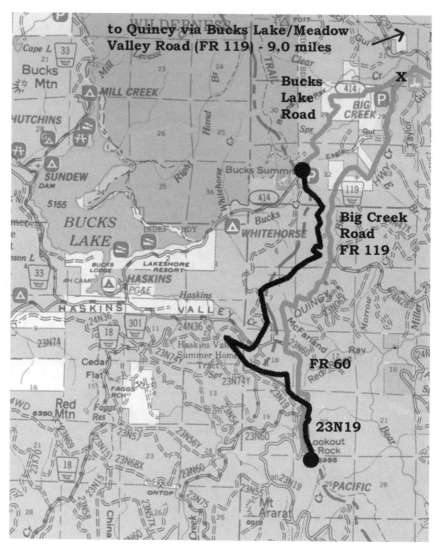

M-7

Hike 8—Bucks Summit to Highway 70 at Belden Town Bridge

PCT: 19.1 miles
Hike: 19.1 miles
Map: M-8 (Plumas NF)
Difficulty: Moderate

🥾 **Hike.** Almost immediately after leaving Bucks Summit (5531), you enter Bucks Lake Wilderness, where you stay for nearly the entire hike. You climb moderately as you work your way N 7.8 miles along the crest

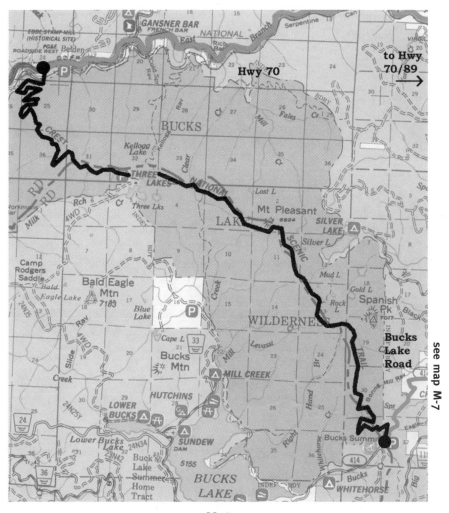

M-8

to a saddle (6710) below the east end of Mt. Pleasant. In the next 2.2 miles, you descend to and parallel Clear Creek, then cross it (6190). In another 1.9 miles, you arrive at a trail (6260) to Three Lakes. Stay on the crest and proceed NW 1.8 miles to the start (5900) of the Belden Trail segment of the PCT, on which you switch your way down 4.7 miles to two railroad tracks (2310). Follow the paved road 0.6 mile to Belden, then cross the bridge (0.1 mile) to Highway 70 (2330).

🚌 **Highway 70 at Belden Town Bridge**. From Bucks Summit, retrace your route to Highway 70/89 in Quincy. Turn left (N) on Highway 70/89 and go 10.1 miles to where Highway 70 departs to the west and Highway 89 continues north. Turn left (W) on Highway 70 and go 18.4 miles to

Belden. There is a PCT TH parking area on the north side of the road just past the bridge that leads into Belden.

Highway 70 near Belden Town Bridge to Burney Falls

Overview

PCT: 134.3 miles
Hikes (11): 135.7 miles
Declination: 16.5° E

In Section N you leave the Sierra Nevada, cross the North Fork Feather River, and arrive at the southernmost peak in the Cascade Range, Lassen Peak, in beautiful Lassen Volcanic National Park. The Cascade Range is a volcanic ridge that runs from Lassen Peak to the Canadian border. One of the peaks in this range, Mt. Saint Helens in Washington State, erupted not very long ago (1980). From Lassen Volcanic National Park, you descend into Hat Creek Valley, traversing along its hot, dry east slope, with views of another volcano, Mt. Shasta, in the distance. From here, you descend to Burney Falls near Lake Britton.

Hike 1—Highway 70 at Belden Town Bridge to FR 26N02 near Humbug Summit

PCT: 17.6 miles
Hike: 17.6 miles
Maps: N-1A, N-1B, and N-1C (Plumas NF)
Difficulty: Difficult
Direction: N→S (Elevation)

🚶 **Hike.** (As of August 1999, from Belden northbound, the PCT was closed. Use the Indian Springs detour.) When the PCT re-opens, you have a strenuous hike up to the crest. That is why we suggest you do it N→S. To be consistent, we describe it S→N.

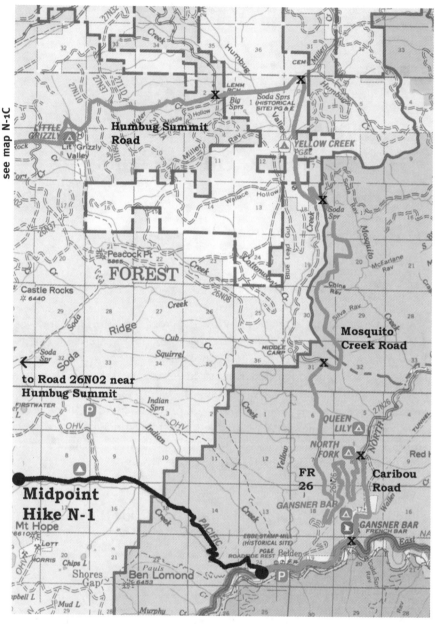

N-1A

Beginning at the Belden TH (2330) by the old Ely Stamp Mill, the PCT parallels Highway 70 for 2.0 miles, crossing a bridge over Indian Creek about halfway. From here, you make a 4.2-mile ascent along Chips Creek to Williams Cabin (3700). Continue W 4.7 miles up along Chips Creek to a creek (5650) that originates from Poison Springs. Traverse around a large bowl and in 2.1 miles you reach Poison Spring itself (6680). Now, climb moderately and follow the crest 4.6 miles to Road 26N02 where it meets 26N04.

🚗 **Highway 70 at Belden Town Bridge**. From Bucks Summit, the starting point of the last hike in Section M, retrace your route to Highway 70/89 in Quincy. Turn left (N) on Highway 70/89 and go 10.1 miles to where Highway 70 departs west and Highway 89 continues north. Turn left (W) on Highway 70 and go 18.4 miles to Belden. There is a PCT TH parking area on the north side of the road just past the bridge that leads into Belden.

🚗 **FR 26N02 near Humbug Summit—best road, longest route from Belden**. (Even though this hike goes through Lassen National Forest, we prefer the Plumas National Forest map, which we show here.) From the PCT TH near the Belden bridge, retrace your route E 17.9 miles on Highway 70 to Highway 89 (not shown on map). Turn left (N) on Highway 89 and go 28.8 miles to Humbug road/Humboldt road south of Chester—see Map N-1B. (Be careful not to confuse the two Hums— Humbug and Humboldt.)

The next part of this drive requires careful attention to detail. From Highway 89, go S 0.6 mile to an unsigned 3-way junction. Humboldt Summit road goes to the right (W) and Humbug Summit road goes straight (S). You go straight (S) 1.2 miles to a signed bridge over Butt Creek. Continue 0.2 mile to an unsigned 4-way junction. To the west, two roads form a **Y**. Take the road to the right (W) and go 0.4 mile along the

Rugged country near Mt. Lassen

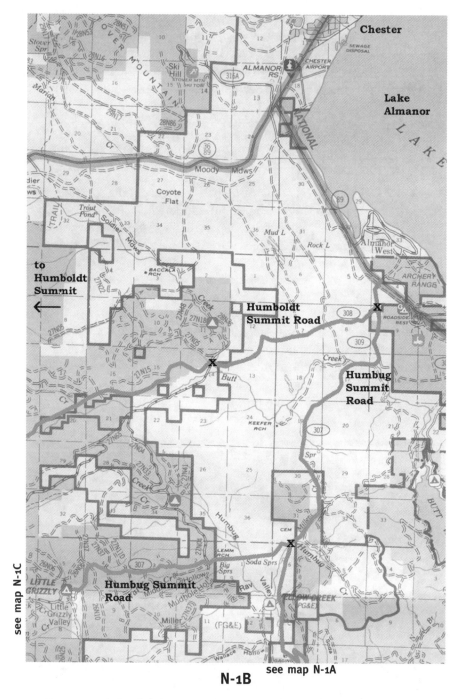

N-1B

see map N-1A

creek to a road that leads to a bridge over the creek to your right. Stay on the same road—don't go over the bridge—for 1.9 miles, staying along the creek, then climbing up to an unsigned four-way junction. Continue SW up 1.0 mile to an obvious crest and an unsigned five-way junction with a large pine tree in the middle of the road. Stop under the tree facing south. The two roads to your left form a very tight **Y**. You want the road to the right, the one that leads SE down the hill 2.3 miles to an unsigned road junction in Humbug Valley near Soda Springs. After this tedious journey, you might think the fun was over, but it is not. (The Soda Springs Historical Marker Site is just south of this junction toward the Yellow Spring CG. If you use the second option, described below, to get to this

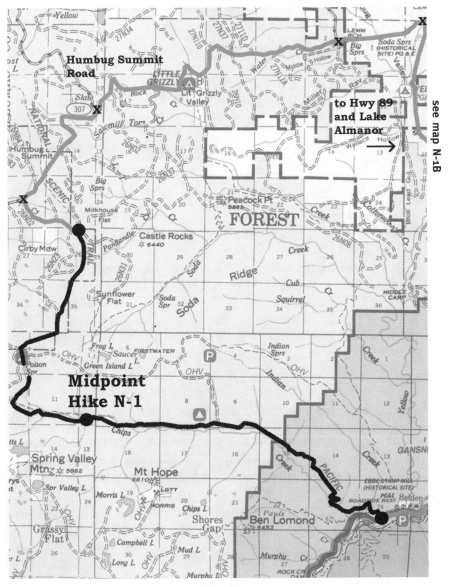

N-1C

junction, you will drive right past the site.) At this junction, you transition from Map N1-B to N-1C.

From the unsigned junction at the east end of Humbug Valley, go W 1.9 miles through broad Humbug Valley to a major road junction and a HUMBUG SUMMIT 9/FANANI MEADOW 6 sign. Follow the sign for Humbug Summit 0.2 mile up to another junction and a HUMBUG SUMMIT LOOP ROAD 9/HUMBUG SUMMIT 10 sign. Turn left (SW) on Humbug Summit road and go 5.0 miles to FR 27N37. At this junction, turn left (W)—you will stay on Humbug Summit road—and go 1.2 miles to the signed entrance to the Little Grizzly CG. Stay on Humbug Summit road and go 1.5 miles to FR 26N35. (We have mentioned all of these roads as check points along this very complicated road system.)

Stay on Humbug Summit road and go 1.8 miles to the junction of FR 26N31/27N65) and a HUMBOLDT VALLEY 8/HUMBUG SUMMIT 2 sign. Follow Humbug Summit road 2.2 miles to the summit, then another 0.5 mile to where the PCT crosses the road near Cold Spring. (You can end this hike here, but it makes the already strenuous hike 1.7 miles longer. Thus, we have chosen to end it at FR 26N02). From the PCT, continue southwest on Humbug Summit road and go 0.7 mile to FR 26N02 and a SUNFLOWER FLAT sign. Turn left (SE) and go 1.6 miles to FR 26N04 and the PCT. The PCT crosses 26N02 at the junction of FRs 26N02/26N04. There are no signs where the PCT crosses 26N02, but the trail itself is obvious on both sides of the road, and there is a rock pile on the north side of the road.

🚐 **FR 26N02 near Humbug Summit—rough dirt road, most direct route from Belden.** Begin with Map N-1A. From the PCT TH near Belden bridge, go E 1.7 miles on Highway 70 to paved Caribou road. Go N 2.0 miles to a bridge across the North Fork Feather River. Turn left (W) and cross the bridge. This dirt road is FR 26. Go 7.7 miles—a lot of up with some stunning views below—to the HUMBUG VALLEY 7/MOSQUITO CREEK 7 sign. Bear right (NE) toward Mosquito Creek. (Do not take Humbug Valley road to the NW unless you have a high clearance 4WD!) From this junction, go 5.3 rough miles to the HUMBUG VALLEY /MOSQUITO CREEK 5/BUTT LAKE 7 sign. Turn left (W) toward Humbug Valley and go 0.7 mile to Lower Yellow Creek road. Turn right (N) toward the campground and go 1.7 miles to the LONGVILLE sign. Go N 1.2 miles toward Longville. You'll pass the Soda Springs Historical Site along the way. At the next unsigned junction, you are at the east end of Humbug Valley.

At this point, you transition from Map N-1A to N-1C. From the unsigned junction at the east end of Humbug Valley, follow the directions to FR 26N02 near Humbug Summit provided in the last two paragraphs of the option entitled "FR 26N02 near Humbug Summit (6380)—best road, longest route from Belden." Whew!

Hike 2—FR 26N02 near Humbug Summit to Humboldt Summit

PCT: 8.5 miles
Hike: 8.5 miles
Map: N-2 (Plumas NF)
Difficulty: Moderate

🚶 **Hike.** From FR 26N02 near Humbug Summit (6380), the PCT goes NW 1.7 miles to Humbug Summit Road 27N01 near Cold Spring (6450). Continue NW 3.2 miles to a jeep road (7000) that drops to Lost Lake. It is another 3.6 miles to Humboldt road at Humboldt Summit (6610).

🚗 **Humboldt Summit.** From the PCT at FR 26N02, retrace your route 1.6 miles to Humbug Summit road. Turn left (SW)—follow the SNAG LAKE 4 sign—and go 0.6 mile to FR 26N27. Turn right on FR 26N27—fol-

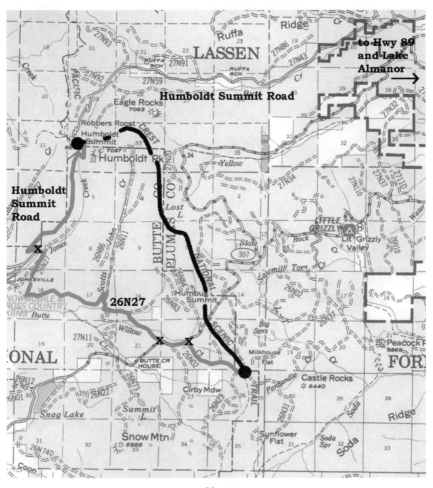

N-2

low the BUTTE MEADOWS 12 sign—and go 5.0 miles to signed Humboldt Summit road. Turn right (N) and go 3.4 rough miles to the summit and the PCT.

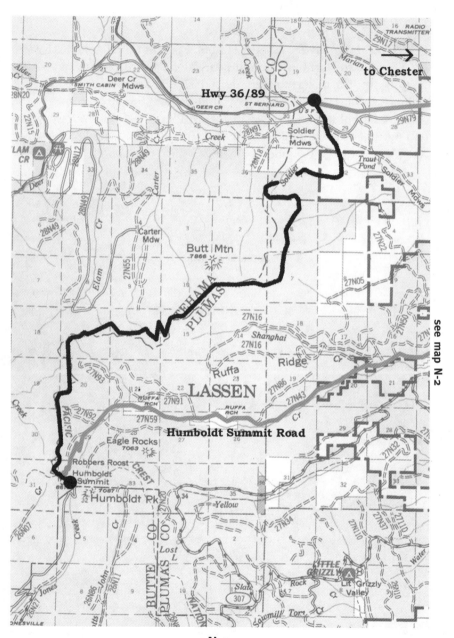

N-3

Hike 3—Humboldt Summit to Highway 36/89

PCT: 20.4 miles
Hike: 20.4 miles
Map: N-3 (Plumas NF)
Difficulty: Difficult

🚶 **Hike.** The first 6.2 miles of the PCT undulate north, then east, along the crest to meet the Carter Meadows Trail on a saddle (6600). Now climb NE 3.7 miles to the Butt Mountain Trail (7590), then descend E, then N, 2.6 miles to a shallow gully (6920). In the next 4.2 miles, you continue to descend, passing the headwaters of Soldier Creek. Then you cross that creek (5480). An easterly 1.5-mile traverse brings you to an old road (5150) where you turn N for the final 2.2 miles to Highway 36/89 (4990).

🚗 **Highway 36/89.** From Humboldt Summit go E 11.5 miles on Humboldt Summit Road to the CHESTER 12/HIGHWAY 89 5 sign. Continue east and go 5.0 miles to the Humboldt-Humbug exit off Highway 89 south of Chester. Turn left (N) on Highway 89 and go 4.3 miles to the junction of Highways 36/89. Turn left (W) on Highway 36/89 and go 5.7 miles to where the PCT crosses the road. There is no place to park here, so continue west 0.4 mile to a logging road that runs SE-NW. Turn left on this road. You can park here, then walk back 0.4 mile east on Highway 36/89, or you can walk SE 0.5 mile down the logging road to the PCT.

Hike 4—Highway 36/89 to Domingo Springs TH

PCT: 9.9 miles
Hike: 9.9 miles
Map: N-4 (Lassen NF)
Difficulty: Easy

🚶 **Hike.** From where the PCT crosses Highway 36/89 (4990), go N 3.2 miles up to Stover Camp (5660). Climb N 2.5 miles to the county-line crest (5920). Continue N 2.3 miles to a logging road (5400) on a ridge, then descend 1.0 mile to a large bridge over North Fork Feather River (5020). A short 0.9-mile hike takes you to the Domingo Springs TH (5110).

🚗 **Domingo Springs TH.** From where the PCT crosses Highway 36/89, retrace your route 5.7 miles to the junction of Highways 36/89 south of Chester. Continue straight (NE) and go 2.6 miles on Highway 36 through the town of Chester to Feather River Drive and a JUNIPER LAKES 13/DRAKESBAD 17 sign. Turn left (W) and go 0.7 mile to an intersection with a JUNIPER LAKES 14/DRAKESBAD 17 sign. Bear left (SW)—follow the sign for Drakesbad—and go 5.4 miles to an intersection with a MINERAL

22/DRAKESBAD 11 sign. Bear left (SW)—follow the sign for Mineral—and go 2.7 miles to the Domingo Springs TH. (The last 0.2 mile of this road is unpaved.)

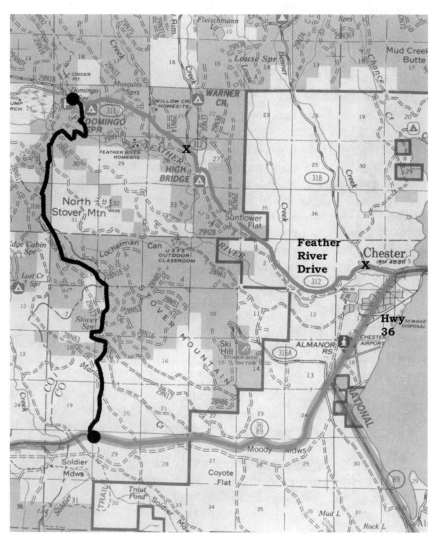

N-4

Mt. Lassen from Drakesbad Road

Hike 5—Domingo Springs TH to Warner Valley CG

PCT: 8.5 miles
Hike: 8.5 miles
Map: N-5 (Lassen NF)
Difficulty: Easy

🚶 **Hike.** From the Domingo Springs TH (5110), climb moderately NW 4.8 miles to the crest, then hike along it to Little Willow Lake (6100). Go N 1.0 mile to a side route (6030) that leads to Terminal Geyser. Turn NW on the PCT and go 1.8 miles to a horse trail (5800). It is another 0.9 mile on the PCT to your destination, the Warner Valley CG (5670).

🚙 **Warner Valley CG.** From the Domingo Springs TH, retrace your route 2.7 miles to the intersection with the sign that reads MINERAL 22/DRAKESBAD 11. At this intersection, turn left (N)—follow the sign for Drakesbad—and go 7.2 miles to where the pavement ends. Continue 3.0 miles on this unpaved road up to the Warner Valley CG and TH. (To get to the Warner Valley CG or Drakesbad Resort, you must pay a $10 fee to enter Lassen Volcanic National Park. Check with the ranger to see how flexible this requirement can be, especially if you are only going to do the day hike we describe here.)

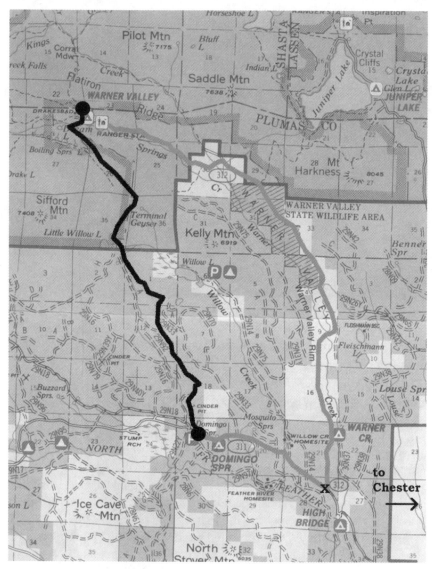

N-5

Hike 6—Warner Valley CG to the East End of Badger Flat

PCT: 13.2 miles
Hike: 13.9 miles
Map: N-6 (Lassen NF)
Difficulty: Moderate

Hike. From the Warner Valley CG (5670) behind campsite #10, the PCT climbs NW 1.0 mile to a trail that leads to several lakes. You turn N on the PCT and go 1.4 miles to a campsite (5990) just before Kings Creek, which you ford. Now parallel Grassy Swale Creek NE 2.5 miles to the first junction with the Horseshoe Lake Trail (6470), another thread of

N-6

see map N-5

which you reach in 1.3 miles further north (6710). Continue N 1.8 miles to the Cluster Lakes Trail (6520). (You could take this trail to Badger Flat. There are lakes, along the way as compared to the dry PCT, and it is slightly shorter.) On the PCT, you go north, then west, 5.2 miles to Badger Flat (6270), Badger Creek, and the north end of the Cluster Lakes Trail. From this junction, go N 0.7 mile along the left (west) side of this N-S creek to FR 32N12. There is no "trail" here, but you can see where several other hikers have gone before you.

👓 **East End of Badger Flat**. No matter how you do it, this day hike involves a lot of driving. In both of the options described below, you must first retrace your route from the Warner Valley CG to Highway 36 in Chester.

The first option takes you west on Highway 36 to Highway 89, which you follow north through Lassen Volcanic National Park. This is a spectacular drive, but it will cost you at least $10 to enter, and drive through, the park. Once through the park, continue north on Highway 89 to Highway 44, from where you can follow the directions in the next paragraph.

The second option takes you from Feather River Drive in Chester E 13.1 miles on Highway 36 to County Road A21. Turn left (N) on A21 and go 18.0 miles to Highway 44. Turn left (NW) on Highway 44 and go 27.7 miles to the junction of Highways 44/89. (You will cross the PCT 0.2 mile east of the junction of Highways 44/89.) Turn left (S) on Highway 89 and go 5.3 miles to FR 32N12. Turn left (SE) on FR 32N12—following the sign TWIN BRIDGES 1/WEST PROSPECT LOOKOUT 12—and go 1.1 miles to the PCT. (This junction is 0.1 mile past the bridge over Hat Creek. It is also where the next hike, Hike 7, ends.) For now, continue SE 5.2 miles on FR 32N12 to a LOOKOUT sign at FR 32N13Y. Follow the LOOKOUT sign 0.3 mile on FR 32N12 down the hill to Badger Creek.

Hike 7—The East End of Badger Flat to Road 32N12 near Twin Bridges CG

PCT: 7.0 miles
Hike: 7.7 miles
Map: N-7 (Lassen NF)
Difficulty: Easy

🚶 **Hike**. From where Badger Creek crosses FR 32N12, hike 0.7 mile along the right (east) side of N-S Badger Creek to where the creek, the PCT, and the Cluster Lakes Trail meet. Go W 2.1 miles to the park boundary (6200) and a trail that leads to Hat Creek. In the next 4.9 miles you cross several roads as you descend parallel to Hat Creek on your way to Road 32N12 (4830) just SE of the bridge that crosses Hat Creek near the Twin Bridges CG.

🚗 **Road 32N12 near Twin Bridges CG.** From the bridge over Badger Creek at the east end of Badger Flat, retrace your route 5.5 miles on FR 32N12 to the PCT. (You are 0.1 mile SE of the bridge over Hat Creek and 1.1 miles SE of Highway 44/89 on FR 32N12.)

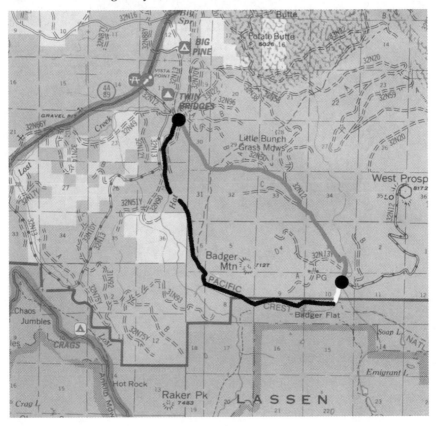

N-7

Hike 8—Road 32N12 near Twin Bridges to Highway 44 TH Parking Area

PCT: 10.3 miles
Hike: 10.3 miles
Map: N-8 (Lassen NF)
Difficulty: Easy

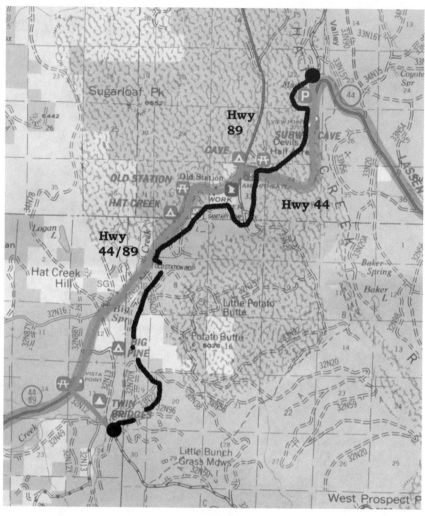

N-8

🥾 **Hike**. From the bridge over Hat Creek (4830), the PCT parallels this creek and Highway 44/89 as it leads north across several dirt roads 8.8 miles to a crossing of Highway 44 (4360). Continue 1.5 miles up to the PCT TH parking area off Highway 44 (4870).

🚗 **Highway 44 TH Parking Area**. From Road 32N12 near the Twin Bridges CG, retrace your route NW 1.1 miles to Highway 44/89. Turn right (N) on Highway 44/89 and go 5.3 miles to where Highway 44 departs to the east. Turn right (E) on Highway 44 and go 2.7 miles to the PCT TH turnoff. Immediately after you make this left turn on to the access road, take a right on FR 34N34 and go 0.4 mile to the TH parking area.

Mt. Lassen from bridge over Hat Creek

Hike 9—Highway 44 TH Parking Area to Road 22

PCT: 13.9 miles
Hike: 13.9 miles
Map: N-9 (Lassen NF)
Difficulty: Moderate

Hike. From the Highway 44 TH parking area (4870), the PCT begins a hot, dry traverse along the east rim of Hat Creek Valley. In 4.3 miles, you pass a short trail (4820) to usually dry Grassy Lake. You stay on the rim for 2.1 miles to a crossing of the upper canyon of Lost Creek (4810). Turn NW on the PCT and go 4.7 miles to Hat Creek Rim Fire Lookout (5122). It is another 2.8 miles to Road 22 (4660).

FR 22. From the Highway 44 TH, retrace your route to the junction of Highways 44/89. Turn right (N) on Highway 89 and go 11.0 miles past the Hat Creek Work Center to paved Doty Road Loop. Turn right (E) and go 1.4 miles to paved Bidwell road. Turn right (E) and go 2.3 miles to unpaved FR 22. Turn left (N) and go 3.7 miles to the PCT, just past an abandoned corral and water tank. If you get to FR 34N18, you have gone 0.1 mile too far.

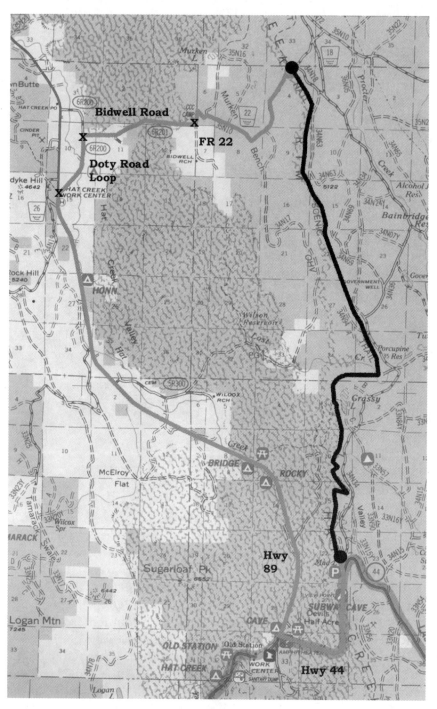

N-9

Hike 10—Road 22 to Highway 299

PCT: 17.3 miles
Hike: 17.3 miles
Map: N-10 (Lassen NF)
Difficulty: Moderate

🥾 **Hike.** This is another hot, dry hike. From Road 22 (4660), you parallel FR 18 for 5.0 miles. Then you make a moderate descent 3.8 miles to a crossing of Cassel-Fall River Mills road (3480). The next 4.4 miles take you to Crystal Lake State Fish Hatchery road (3000). In the last 4.1-mile segment of this hike, you follow Hat Creek for a mile before turning west to Highway 299 (3110).

🚐 **Highway 299.** From FR 22, retrace your route to Highway 89. Turn right (N) and go 10.5 miles to Highway 299. Turn right (NE) and go 2.2 miles to Cassel road, where you can park. The PCT is 0.1 mile further west on Highway 299.

Hat Creek Radio Astronomy Observatory near FR 22

Hike 11—Highway 299 to Burney Falls

PCT: 7.7 miles
Hike: 7.7 miles
Map: N-11 (Lassen NF)
Difficulty: Easy

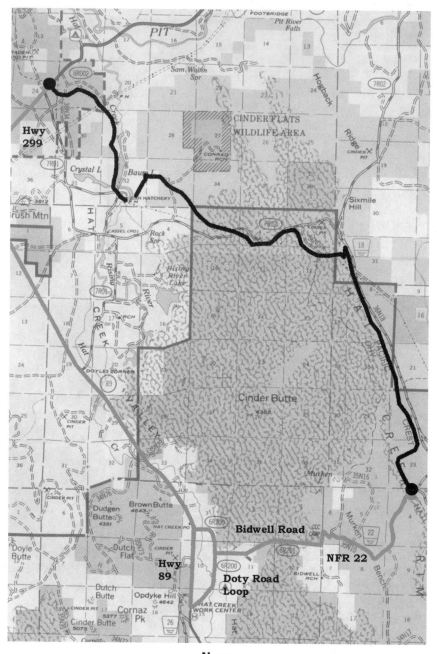

N-10

👤 **Hike**. From Highway 299 (3110), you cross several roads before arriving 3.6 miles later at Arkright Flat (2995). In 1.6 more miles you cross Rim of Lake road (3010), then in another 1.5 miles reach Highway 89

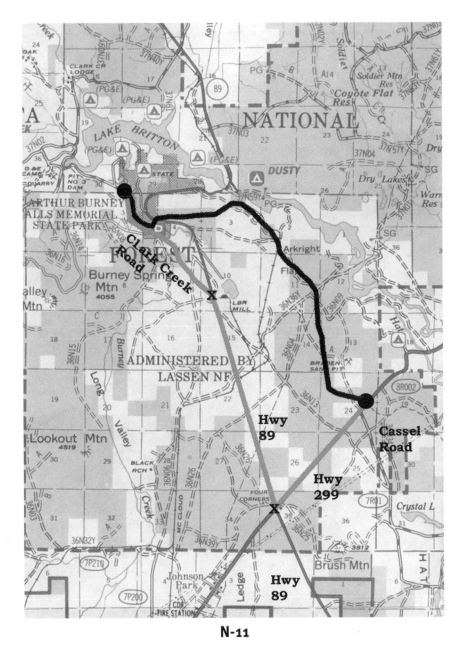

N-11

(2995). Cross Highway 89 and in 1.0 mile arrive at a small parking area (2970) on Clark Creek road near a trail that leads to Burney Falls.

🚗 **Burney Falls.** Retrace your route on Highway 299 to Highway 89. Turn right (N) and go 4.3 miles to paved Clark Creek road. Turn left (NW) and go 1.7 miles to a small TH parking area and a broad path that leads 50 yards east to the PCT. (There is no parking at this TH from 8 P.M. to 6

A.M. You can also end the hike inside Burney Falls SP, 1.6 miles north of Clark Creek road on Highway 89, but it will cost you $5 to enter the park. You can also end it where the PCT crosses Highway 89, 1.2 miles north of Clark Creek road. Here you can park for free. If you park here, however, you have to hike west 1.0 mile to reach the TH at the end of Section N, or you will have to add 1.0 mile to the beginning of Section O. No matter where you begin or end the hike, a side trip to Burney Falls itself is most rewarding.)

Burney Falls to Interstate 5 near Castle Crags SP

Overview

PCT: 82.9 miles
Hikes (7): 82.9 miles
Declination: 16.75° E

Y ou hike through dense forests created by more-than-abundant rainfall. This is a prime logging area. Along the way, there are spectacular views of Mt. Shasta to the north.

Hike 1—Burney Falls to FR 37 above Rock Creek

PCT: 5.8 miles
Hike: 5.8 miles
Map: O-1 (Shasta-Trinity NF)
Difficulty: Easy

🥾 **Hike.** This is a short hike, one you can use to introduce friends to the PCT. If it is too short, you can combine it with the next hike (8.3 miles) to make it longer (14.1 miles). From the parking area adjacent to Clark Creek road (2950), hike west 1.9 miles to the Lake Britton dam (2760). Then undulate W 3.5 miles to Rock Creek (2980). From here, go up 0.4 mile to FR 37.

🚗 **Burney Falls.** From where the last hike in Section N began, retrace your route on Highway 299 to Highway 89 near the town of Burney. Turn right (N) on Highway 89 and go 4.3 miles to paved Clark Creek road. Turn left (NW) and go 1.7 miles to a small TH parking area and a broad path that leads 50 yards east to the PCT. (There is no parking at this TH from 8 P.M. to 6 A.M. You can also end the hike inside Burney Falls SP, 1.6 miles north of Clark Creek road on Highway 89, but it will cost you $5 to

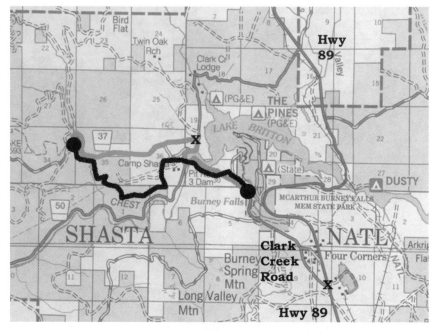

O-1

enter the park. You can also end it where the PCT crosses Highway 89, 1.2
miles north of Clark Creek road. Here you can park for free. If you park
here, however, you have to hike west 1.0 mile to reach the TH at end of
Section N, or you will have to add 1.0 mile to the beginning of Section O.
No matter where you begin or end the hike, a side trip to Burney Falls is
most rewarding.)

🚗 **FR 37 above Rock Creek**. From the TH parking area on Clark
Creek road, turn right (NW) on paved Clark Creek road and go 2.1 miles
past the Lake Britton dam to a 4-way intersection. Turn left (W) on FR
37—do not follow signs for Highway 89—and go 0.5 mile to where the
pavement ends. Continue straight (W) on unpaved FR 37 and go 2.1 miles
to Rock Creek. Cross the creek and go up 0.3 mile on FR 37 to where the
PCT crosses FR 37.

Hike 2—FR 37 above Rock Creek to Peavine Creek

PCT: 8.3 miles
Hike: 8.3 miles
Map: O-2 (Shasta-Trinity NF)
Difficulty: Easy
Direction: N→S (Elevation)

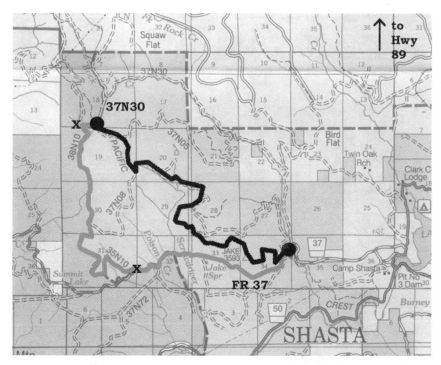

O-2

🚶 **Hike**. From FR 37 above Rock Creek (3100), you wind W 4.3 miles up to a road junction (4480). Go NE 0.7 mile to another road crossing, then another 0.7 mile to the edge of an old clearcut (4660). Turn W and go 2.6 miles to a road junction just before Peavine Creek (4760).

🚗 **Peavine Creek**. From where the PCT crosses FR 37 above Rock Creek, go SW 3.4 miles on partly paved FR 37 to dirt FR 38N10. Turn right (N) and go 4.9 miles to a 3-way junction with FR 37N30. Turn right (E) and go 0.3 mile to Peavine Creek and the PCT.

Hike 3—Peavine Creek to the Logging Road East of Bartle Gap

PCT: 12.0 miles
Hike: 12.0 miles
Map: O-3 (Shasta-Trinity NF)
Difficulty: Moderate

🚶 **Hike**. From Peavine Creek (4760), hike NW 1.6 miles up to some huge power lines (5200). Go N 1.2 miles to the base of Red Mountain (5380). Continuing N 3.8 miles, you intersect Road 38N10 (5410) near the

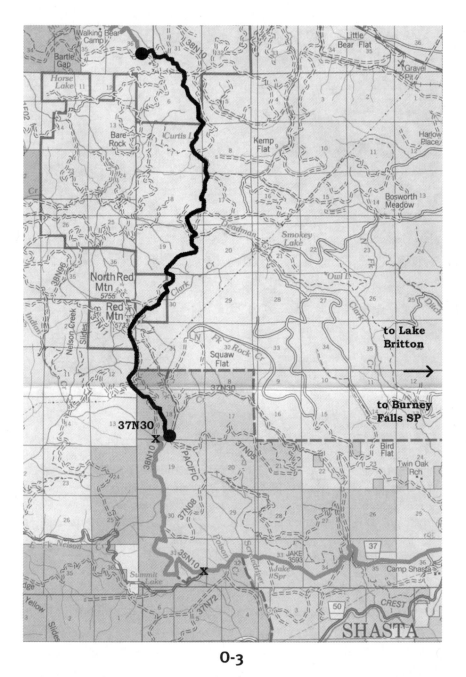

O-3

headwaters of Deadman Creek. Still northbound, in 3.2 more miles you turn west and follow 38N10 for the last 2.2 miles to a logging road east of Bartle Gap.

🚐 **Logging Road East of Bartle Gap**. From Peavine Creek, retrace your route to the junction of Clark Creek road and FR 37 near the Lake Britton dam. Turn left (N) on Clark Creek road—follow the HIGHWAY 89 3 sign—and go 3.7 miles to Highway 89. Turn left (N) on Highway 89 and go 15.9 miles (just past Dead Horse Summit) to unpaved FR 39N05 (Bartle Gap road). Turn left (S) and go 4.4 miles to the junction of FR 39N05 and a logging road. (From this point, FR 39N05 to Bartle Gap is a high-clearance 4WD road only.) Turn left (SE) and go 1.1 miles up the logging road to where it meets FR 38N10 on the crest. Park at this intersection. Walk 250 yards (0.15 mile) down the log road to the right (bearing 080°)—do not follow 38N10—to the PCT.

Hike 4—Logging Road East of Bartle Gap to Grizzly Peak Lookout Road 39N06

PCT: 16.0 miles
Hike: 16.0 miles
Map: O-4 (Shasta-Trinity NF)
Difficulty: Moderate

🥾 **Hike**. From the logging road (5110), go W 1.6 miles to Bartle Gap (5070). Continue W 4.0 miles to a rocky point (6080) near Mushroom Rock, then parallel FR 38N10 for 5.1 miles in a moderate descent to the

Mt. Shasta in winter

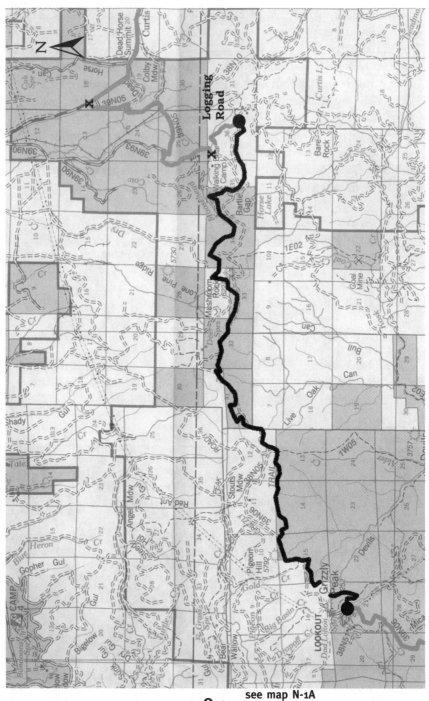

see map N-1A
O-4

Alder Creek Trail (5440). It is another 5.3 miles to Grizzly Peak Lookout Road 39N06 (5640).

🚗 **Grizzly Peak Lookout Road 39N06**. From the logging road east of Bartle Gap, retrace your route to Highway 89. Turn left (N) on Highway 89 and go 19.8 miles to Squaw Valley road in the town of McCloud. Turn left (S)—follow the sign for MCLOUD RESERVOIR 10—and go 5.1 miles on paved Squaw Valley road to where it becomes FR 11. Staying on FR 11, you go another 0.9 mile to FR 39N21. (This junction will be relevant in the directions to the end of Hike 6.) For now, stay on FR 11 and go 5.5 miles to FR 38N53. (This junction will be relevant in the directions to the beginning of Hike 6.) For now, stay on FR 11 and go 3.1 miles to where the pavement ends. Still on now-dirt and now rough FR 11, go 4.8 miles to signed Grizzly Peak Lookout Road 39N06. Turn left (N) on FR 39N06 and go up 4.9 miles to a saddle where four roads meet under some power lines. Continue straight (N) and go up 0.3 mile to a saddle where the PCT crosses FR 39N06. (Vandals have trashed the road markers at the saddle intersection under the power lines. For a nice view of Mt. Shasta, continue up FR 39N06 to the Grizzly Peak Lookout.)

Hike 5—Grizzly Peak Lookout Road 39N06 to Ah-Di-Na CG Road 38N53

PCT: 12.8 miles
Hike: 12.8 miles
Map: O-5 (Shasta-Trinity NF)
Difficulty: Moderate

🚶 **Hike**. From Grizzly Peak Lookout road (5540), you follow Deer Creek down for 3.5 miles to a side canyon (4360). In the next 3.2 miles you descend to and cross Butcherknife Creek (3300), which feeds Deer Creek below it. Still descending, you reach McCloud-Big Bend road (2404) in 3.4 miles. The final 2.7 miles take you across the McCloud River via a bridge, then on to FR 38N53 (2400) near the Ah-Di-Na CG and historical site.

🚗 **Ah-Di-Na CG Road 38N53**. From Grizzly Peak Lookout, retrace your route to FR 11. Now, retrace your route 4.8 rough miles along FR 11 to where the pavement begins. Staying on FR 11, you cross McCloud Lake dam and in 3.1 miles arrive at FR 38N53. Turn left (SW) on rough dirt FR 38N53—follow the AH-DI-NA 6 sign—and go 5.6 miles to the PCT. The CG and historical site at Ah-Di-Na are 0.6 mile further down FR 38N53.

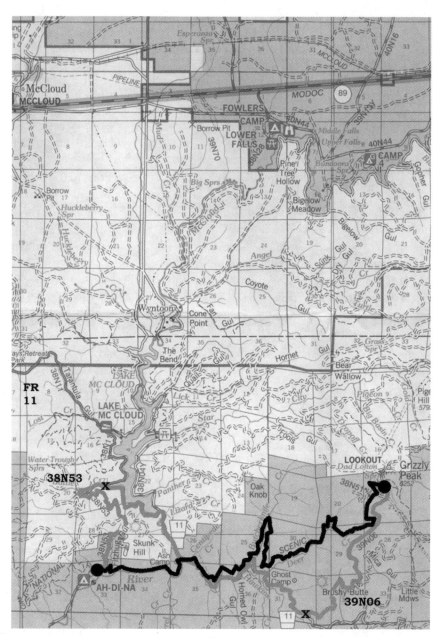

O-5

Hike 6—Ah-Di-Na CG Road 38N53 to Road Junction and Saddle near Cabin Creek TH

PCT: 12.0 miles
Hike: 12.0 miles
Map: O-6 (Shasta-Trinity NF)
Difficulty: Moderate

🥾 **Hike.** From the junction of the PCT and FR 38N53 (2400), the PCT climbs gradually 3.1 miles to where it intersects Bald Mountain road (3380). From here, the PCT undulates N 2.7 miles to a ridge saddle (3880), then turns W and goes 2.1 miles to Trough Creek (3030). Continue W 3.2 miles to Squaw Valley Creek (2580), then climb 0.9 mile out of the canyon to a saddle with three roads converging on it (3059)

🚙 **Road Junction and Saddle near Cabin Creek TH**. From Ah-Di-Na, retrace your route on FR 38N53 to FR 11. Turn left (N) on FR 11 and go 5.5 miles to dirt FR 39N21. Turn left (S) and go 3.0 miles to the Cabin Creek TH. Turn right (W), staying on the same road, and go 0.6 mile to a road junction just after crossing Cabin Creek. Continue straight (S) and go 0.7 mile up the hill to a saddle where four roads and the PCT converge.

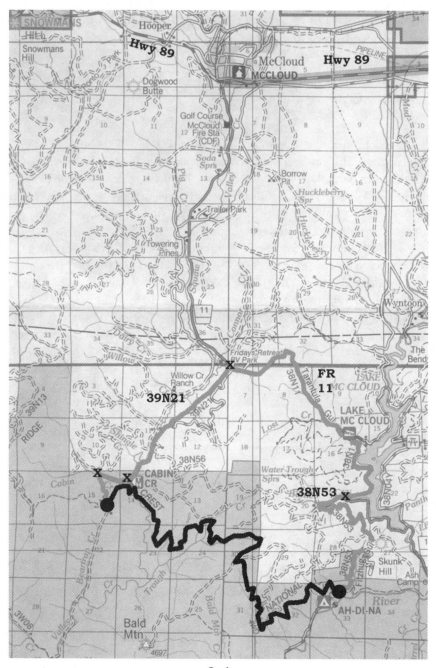

O-6

Hike 7—Road Junction and Saddle near Cabin Creek TH to I-5 near Castle Crags SP

PCT: 16.0 miles
Hike: 16.0 miles
Map: O-7 (Shasta-Trinity NF)
Difficulty: Moderate

Hike. From the road junction and saddle (3059) near Cabin Creek TH, go W 4.8 miles as you climb to Girard Ridge Road 39N13 (4600). Now work your way around private property 4.9 miles to Fall Creek (4050). Parallel the creek 1.5 miles down to a road (3770) and the boundary of Castle Crags SP. It is another 4.1 miles down to Riverside road (2180). Follow this road W 0.7 mile over the Sacramento River, across the railroad tracks, and under I-5 to the east boundary of the west half of Castle Crags SP (2130).

I-5 near Castle Crags SP. From Cabin Creek, retrace your route on FR 39N21 to FR 11. Turn left (N) and go 6.0 miles to Highway 89 in McCloud. Turn left (W) and go 9.7 miles to Highway I-5. Go S 9.8 miles on Highway I-5 to the Soda Creek road exit. The PCT segment ends 0.1 mile west of the exit at the east boundary of the west half of Castle Crags State Park, where you are greeted with a NO PARKING ANYTIME sign. To park, turn around and go E 0.3 mile on Soda Creek road—also the PCT at this point—under Highway I-5 and across the railroad tracks. You can park on either side of the road.

Lodging and dining tips in McCloud. You can find excellent American and Mexican food at the Briarpatch Restaurant, 140 Squaw Valley Road (530) 964-2653. There are several lodging options in McCloud. One is the McCloud River Lodge (530) 964-2700, which is adjacent to the Briarpatch Restaurant and has five rooms to rent. The McCloud Timer Inn, 153 Squaw Valley Road (530) 964-2893, is a traditional motel that rents rooms for $40-45. For those who want a historic B&B experience, we recommend the McCloud Hotel, 408 Main Street (530) 964-2844; e-mail: mchotel@snowcrest.net. For a less expensive B&B, try the Stoney Brook Inn, 309 W. Colombero (530) 964-2300. We stayed at this inn twice and were pleased with the rooms, the service, and the hot tub. However, we learned that the inn is for sale, so we cannot vouch for what it may offer in the future.

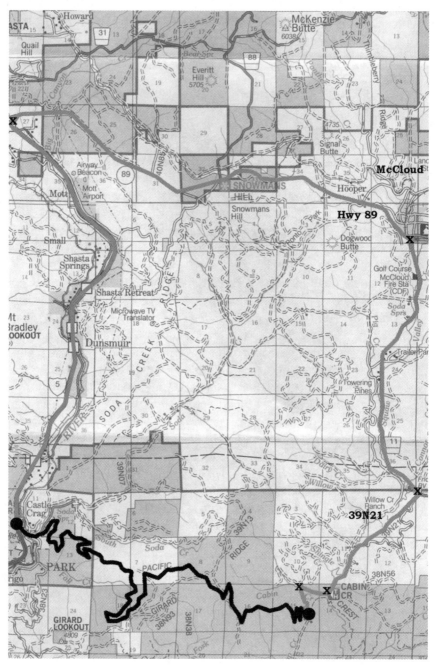

O-7

Interstate 5 near Castle Crags SP to Etna Summit

Overview

PCT: 99.8 miles
Hikes (7): 103.4 miles
Declination: 17° E

Section P climbs from Castle Crags SP (2130) to the 6000-7000 foot crest, where it stays for most of this section. There are several lakes in this section, but most are located in deep basins that are difficult to descend to, particularly in early season when snow is a factor. The section is heavily forested and you will see evidence of logging activity—a plethora of logging roads, which give day hikers a lot of access points to the PCT.

Hike 1—Castle Crags SP to Dog Trail West of Sulphur Creek

PCT: 7.2 miles
Hike: 7.9 miles
Map: P-1 (Shasta-Trinity NF)
Difficulty: Easy

🚶 **Hike.** From the east entrance to Castle Crags SP (2130), you hike S 0.5 mile to the Kettlebelly Trail (2420), which you follow through Castle Crags SP. In 1.3 miles you pass the Root Creek Trail (2590) and in another 0.7 mile, the Bobs Hat Trail (2820). In another 1.0 mile you bridge Winton Canyon Creek (2875), then work your way NW 3.1 miles to Sulphur Creek (2750). Continue 0.6 mile to the Dog Trail (3040), where you leave the PCT. Go SW 0.4 mile on the Dog Trail, then dog-leg SE 0.3 mile to the unsigned TH, which is nothing more than a gravel pit.

🚗 **I-5 near Castle Crags SP.** From the Cabin Creek TH, the starting point of the last hike in Section O, retrace your route to FR 11. Turn left

(N) on FR 11 and go 6.0 miles to Highway 89 in McCloud. Turn left (W) and go 9.7 miles to Highway I-5. Go S 9.8 miles on Highway I-5 to the Soda Creek exit. The PCT segment ends 0.1 mile west of the exit at the east boundary of the west half of Castle Crags State Park, where you are greeted with a NO PARKING ANYTIME sign. To park, turn around and go E 0.3 mile on Soda Creek road—also the PCT at this point—under Highway I-5 and across the railroad tracks. You can park on either side of the road.

🚙 **Dog Trail west of Sulphur Creek.** From the east boundary of the west half of Castle Crags SP at the Soda Creek exit off Highway I-5, go S 2.1 miles on Frontage Road to Castle Creek road. Go W 2.7 miles on Castle Creek road to where this road becomes paved FR 25. Continue W 0.6 mile on FR 25 to a gravel pit on the north side of the road. This is the unsigned Dog Trail TH parking area. (If you reach the North Fork Castle Creek, you have gone 0.3 mile past the TH.) Park in the gravel pit. Take a bearing of 330°—you can see the trail going up a gully—and go up 0.3 mile to where the Dog Trail dog-legs to the right—bearing 060°. Continue up 0.4 miles to the PCT.

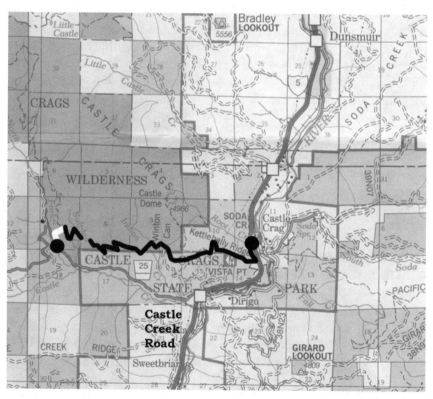

P-1

Castle Crags SP

Hike 2—Dog Trail West of Sulphur Creek to Gumboot TH

PCT: 17.5 miles
Hike: 18.2 miles
Map: P-2 (Shasta-Trinity NF)
Difficulty: Moderate

Hike. The Dog Trail leaves the gravel pit (see above) at a bearing of 330° and goes up 0.3 mile to where it dog-legs to the right—bearing 060°—for another 0.4-mile climb to the PCT (3040). Snake your way NW 2.8 miles to North Fork Castle Creek (3370). You climb over 2000 feet in the next 4.0 miles to the headwaters of North Fork Castle Creek (5750). Contour 1.0 mile around the ridge to yet another creek (5840), then go 3.2 miles along the ridge to the Soapstone Trail (6500). Hike W 4.2 miles to the Trinity Divide (6780), then NW 2.3 miles to the Gumboot TH on Road 40N30 (6460).

Gumboot TH—via good FR Roads. From the Dog Trail TH, go W 7.6 miles on FR 25 to where the pavement ends. Continue SW 1.5 miles on FR 25 to FR 26. Bear right (W) on dirt FR 26 and go 4.9 miles to where pavement begins. Continue N 3.4 miles to the Gumboot TH.

Gumboot TH—via paved roads under construction. (Hopefully, by the time you read this, this option will be completed. The Forest Service is repairing a paved road in the area. However, even if it is not completed, there is a dirt road option.) From the Dog Trail, retrace your

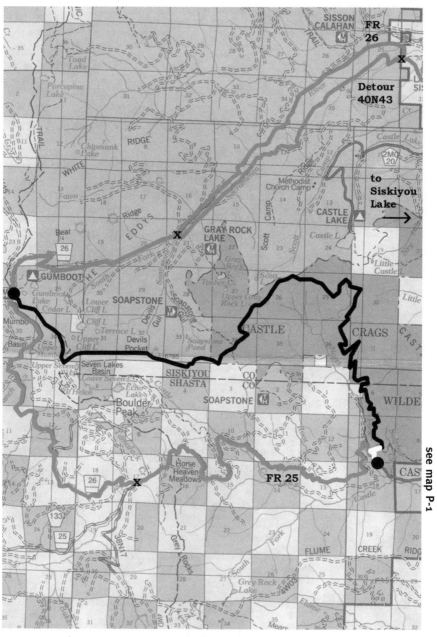

P-2

route on Castle Creek road to the Castella exit off I-5, an exit you passed
when you came from the Soda Creek exit. Go N 13.6 miles on I-5 to the
Central Mt. Shasta exit. Follow the sign for Siskiyou Lake and go W 0.3
mile on Hatchery Lane to a stop sign. Turn left (S) and go 0.2 mile to W. A.

George and Pat at Castle Crags SP; Mount Shasta in the background

Barr road. Bear right (S) on W. A. Barr—again, follow the signs for Siskiyou Lake—and go 4.9 miles around the lake to FR 40N43, a by-pass road that was in use in 1999. If FR 26 is still closed, use FR 40N43 as the detour and follow the directions given below. If FR 26 is open, follow it to the Gumboot TH.

If FR 26 is closed, turn left (NW) on the detour (FR 40N43) and go 0.8 mile to where the pavement ends. Continue NW 5.8 miles on this some-times paved, rough road to where it reunites with paved FR 26 just north of Fawn Creek. Turn left on FR 26 and go 3.6 miles to a junction with the Gumboot CG road. Bear right (W) on FR 26 and go 2.4 miles to the crest and the Gumboot TH.

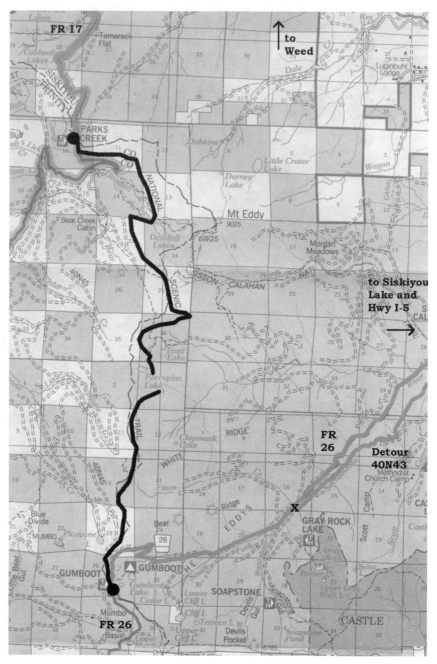

P-3

Hike 3—Gumboot TH to Parks Creek Road TH

PCT: 14.3 miles
Hike: 14.3 miles
Map: P-3 (Shasta-Trinity NF)
Difficulty: Moderate

🚶 **Hike.** From the Gumboot TH (6460), the PCT turns north and follows the Trinity/Siskiyou County Line 5.6 miles to the Porcupine Lake spur trail (7220). Continue N 5.7 miles past Toad Lake to the Deadfall Lakes Trail (7230). Go N 1.4 miles to a spring (7080), then turn W 1.6 miles to Parks Creek Road TH (6830).

🚐 **Parks Creek Road TH.** Depending on which route you followed to get to the Gumboot TH, retrace your route to the Central Mt. Shasta exit off I-5. Go N 12.0 miles on I-5 to the Edgewood/Gazelle exit. Go W 0.1 mile to Old Highway 99. Turn right (N)—follow the sign for Stewart Spring Road—and go 0.4 mile to paved Stewart Spring Road. Turn left (SW) on Stewart Spring road and go 3.9 miles to paved FR 17, which you follow 9.3 miles to the Parks Creek TH.

Hike 4—Parks Creek Road TH to Fen TH near Kangaroo Lake

PCT: 10.9 miles
Hike: 12.0 miles
Map: P-4 (Klamath NF)
Difficulty: Moderate

🚶 **Hike.** From Parks Creek Road TH (6830), go NW 3.0 miles around Cement Bluff to a meadow (6770), then wind SW 3.3 miles to Chilcoot Creek (6650). Turn W 2.1 miles to a saddle (7100) near Bull Lake. Continue W 2.5 miles to a ridge above Kangaroo Lake and the Sisson-Callahan Trail (6480), which descends 1.1 miles to the Fen TH on Kangaroo Lake Road 41N08.

🚐 **Kangaroo Lake—northerly route.** Retrace your route from the Parks Creek TH to the junction of Stewart Spring road and Old Highway 99 near the Edgewood/Gazelle exit off I-5. Turn left (N) on Old Highway 99 and go 7.6 miles to the Gazelle-Callahan Road. Turn left (W) and go 16.6 miles to Rail Creek Road—FR 41N08. Turn left (S) and go 6.7 miles to the Fen TH near Kangaroo Lake. TH parking and the Kangaroo Lake CG are 0.1 mile further.

🚐 **Kangaroo Lake—southerly route.** From the Parks Creek TH, go S 13.4 miles on mostly paved FR 17 to Highway 3. Turn right (NW) and go 5.4 miles to the Scott Mountain TH. (This TH is where the next hike, Hike

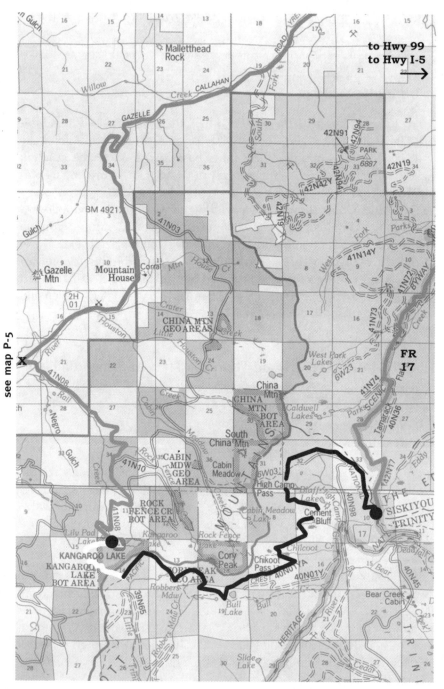

P-4

5, ends.) Continue straight (NW) on Highway 3 6.5 miles to Gazelle-Callahan road. Turn right (NE) and go 8.5 miles to Rail Creek road—FR 41N08. Turn right (S) and go 6.7 miles to the Fen TH near Kangaroo Lake. TH parking and the Kangaroo Lake CG are 0.1 mile further.

Hike 5—Fen TH near Kangaroo Lake to Scott Mountain Summit at Highway 3

PCT: 9.8 miles
Hike: 10.9 miles
Map: P-5 (Klamath NF)
Difficulty: Moderate

🥾 **Hike.** From the Fen TH near Kangaroo Lake road, hike 1.1 miles up the Sisson-Callahan Trail to the PCT (6480). The PCT assumes a southerly direction as you hike parallel to and above the Little Trinity River. At 3.5 miles, you pass two springs (6080), and in 2.0 more miles reach the Grouse Creek Trail (6130). Go 1.1 miles to Masterson Meadow Lake (6180), then descend gradually 3.2 miles to Highway 3 (5401) near Scott Mountain Summit.

🚐 **Scott Mountain Summit at Highway 3.** From the Fen TH near the Kangaroo Lake CG, retrace your route 6.8 miles on FR 41N08 to Gazelle-Callahan Road. Turn left (SW) and go 8.5 miles to Highway 3. Turn left (SE) and go 6.5 miles to the Scott Mountain Summit TH.

Kangaroo Lake from PCT

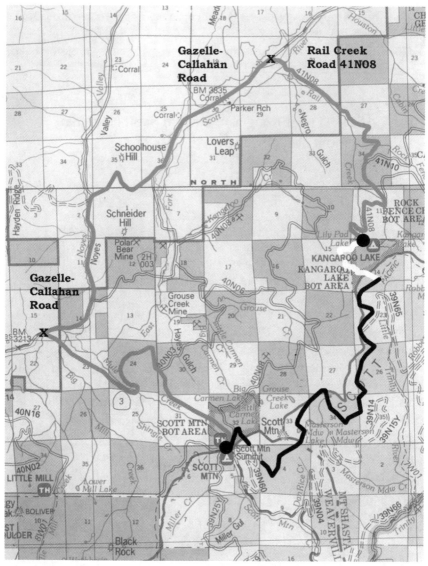

P-5

Hike 6—Scott Mountain Summit at Highway 3 to Carter Summit TH at FR 93

PCT: 19.9 miles
Hike: 19.9 miles
Map: P-6 (Klamath NF)
Difficulty: Moderate

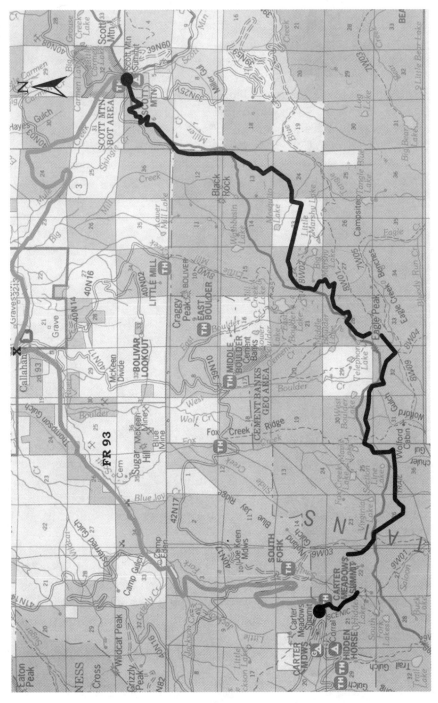

P-6

🥾 **Hike**. From Highway 3 (5401) near Scott Mountain Summit, hike SW 2.8 miles to the boundary of Trinity Alps Wilderness (6370). You hike along FR 40N63 for the next 3.3 miles to Mosquito Lake Creek (6240). Turn W 2.0 miles to the East Boulder Lake Trail/Marshy Lakes Trail saddle (7020). Go SW 3.5 miles to Bloody Run Trail 8W04 (7160), then 2.5 miles to Trail 8W07 (7230), which descends to Fox Creek Lake. Turn west and descend 4.9 miles to South Fork Scott River (5780). Climb from the river NW 0.9 mile to Carter Meadows Summit at FR 93 (6160).

🚐 **Carter Meadows Summit at FR 93**. From Scott Mountain Summit, retrace your route 6.5 miles on Highway 3 to the Gazelle-Callahan Road. Turn left (W) on Highway 3 and go 1.9 miles through the village of Callahan to unsigned FR 93. Turn left (SW) on paved FR 93—follow the CECILVILLE 30 sign—and go 11.7 miles to the tiny Carter Summit TH, which is just off the highway on a rough 100-yard access road next to a helicopter landing pad.

Hike 7—Carter Summit TH at FR 93 to Etna Summit at FR 1C01

PCT: 20.2 miles
Hike: 20.2 miles
Map: P-7A and P-7B (Klamath NF)
Difficulty: Difficult

🥾 **Hike**. From Carter Meadows Summit at FR 93 (6160), hike NW 5.1 miles to the first of two jeep trails (6940). Go N 2.0 miles to the outlet creek of Bingham Lake (6940), then continue N 5.0 miles across several creeks to Trail 9W09, which leads down to FR 40N54. In another 2.2 miles, you reach Paynes Lake's outlet creek (6460). Now, work your way NW 5.9 miles to Etna Summit and paved FR 1C01.

🚐 **Etna Summit**. From the Carter Summit TH, retrace your route 11.7 miles on FR 93 to Highway 3 near the village of Callahan. Turn left (NW) on Highway 3 and go 12.0 miles to the MAIN ST sign for the town of Etna, home of the Etna Brewing Company. Turn left (S) on Main Street and go 0.4 mile to Collier Way in the middle of town. (This intersection will be important in getting to the end of Hike 1 in Section Q). Continue S on Main Street 10.1 miles on this steep, paved road to Etna Summit. TH parking is 0.1 mile past the summit.

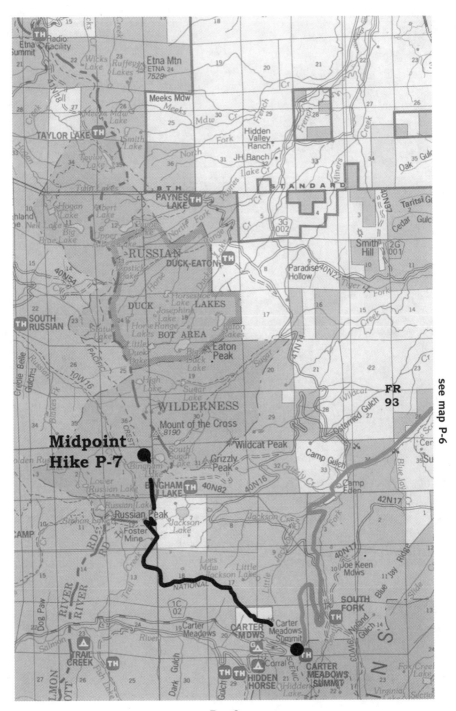

P-7A

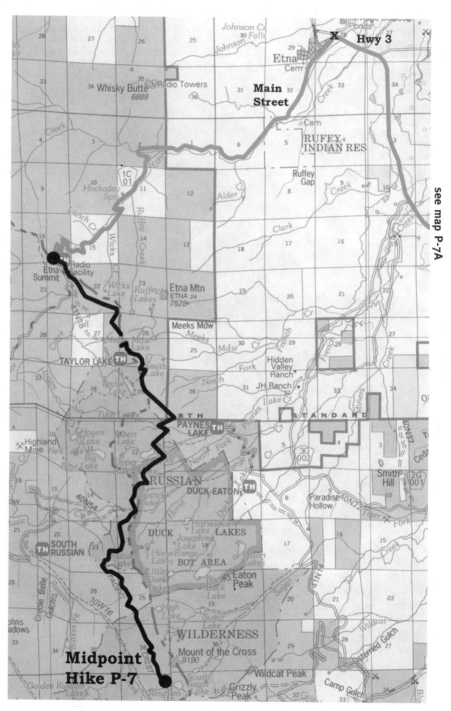

P-7B

Etna Summit to Seiad Valley

Overview

PCT: 56.8 miles
Hikes (5): 76.2 miles
Declination: 17.25° E

From beautiful Etna Summit (5960), the first 37 miles of Section Q stay on the crest. You pass through Marble Mountain Wilderness, then gradually descend via Grider Canyon to quiet Seiad Valley (1371).

Hike 1—Etna Summit at FR 1C01 to 4WD Road near Kidder Creek TH

PCT: 15.6 miles
Hike: 21.0 miles
Map: Q-1 (Klamath NF)
Difficulty: Moderate
Direction: S→N (Elevation)

🚶 **Hike.** From Etna Summit (5960), ascend NW 3.7 miles to the beginning of Razor Ridge (6690). Stay on the PCT and go N 3.9 miles to Babs Fork Kidder Creek (6290). Now, still on the PCT, traverse the ridge NW 3.1 miles to the outlet creek of Shelly Lake (6150), then go 0.5 mile to the Shelly Fork Trail (6340). Go NW on the PCT 2.9 miles to tiny Fisher Lake (6220), then 1.5 miles to a trail junction (6560). At this point, you leave the PCT and go N 0.4 mile to the Kidder Lake Trail, which you follow steeply down 750 feet in 1.1 miles to Kidder Lake. Continue E 2.4 miles down the Kidder Creek Trail to its unsigned TH, then E 1.5 miles on the 4WD-only road to a small parking area at a road junction.

🚗 **Etna Summit.** From the Carter Summit TH, the starting point for the last hike in Section P, retrace your route 11.7 miles on FR 93 to Highway 3 near the village of Callahan. Turn left (NW) on Highway 3

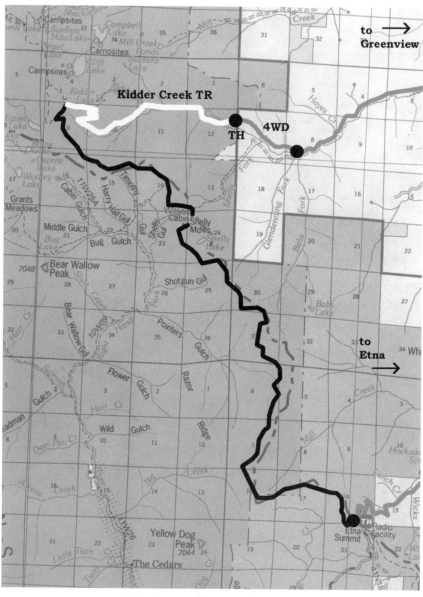

Q-1

and go 12.0 miles to the MAIN ST sign for the town of Etna, home of the Etna Brewing Company. Turn left (S) on Main Street and go 0.4 mile to Collier Way in the middle of town. (This intersection will be important in getting to the end of this hike). Continue S on Main Street 10.1 miles on this steep, paved road to Etna Summit. TH parking is 0.1 mile past the summit.

Etna Valley on the way to Etna Summit

🚙 **4WD Road near Kidder Creek TH**. From Etna Summit, retrace your route 10.1 miles to Collier Way in the center of Etna. Go N 0.5 mile on Collier Way to Highway 3. Bear left (N) on Highway 3 and go 6.3 miles to Quartz Valley Road in Greenview. Turn left (SW) and go 0.4 mile into town to First St. Turn left (S) and go 0.2 mile to paved N Kidder Creek Road. Turn right (W) and go 3.5 miles to where the pavement ends. Continue W 1.6 miles on this now-dirt road to an unsigned junction. Bear left (SW) and go 0.8 mile to another unsigned junction. Bear right (NW) and go up 2.4 miles on this rough dirt road, paralleling Kidder Creek, to yet another unsigned junction. Hike W 1.5 miles on this 4WD-only road to the unsigned Kidder Creek TH.

Hike 2—4WD Road near Kidder Creek TH to Lovers Camp TH

PCT: 8.5 miles
Hike: 17.9 miles
Map: Q-2 (Klamath NF)
Difficulty: Moderate

🥾 **Hike**. We debated this hike, and the next one, for a long time. Each hike is long for yielding such a short piece of the PCT. On the other hand, they help us achieve our goal—day hikes that give more people a chance to experience the beauty of the PCT.

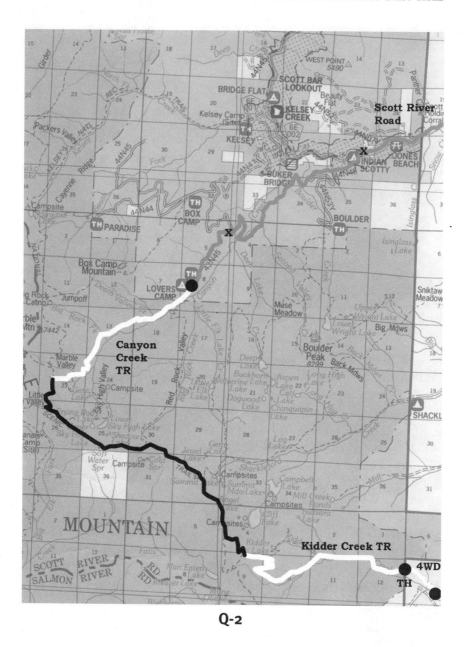

Q-2

To begin, hike up the 4WD road 1.5 miles to the unsigned Kidder Creek TH. Follow the Kidder Creek Trail 2.4 miles to Kidder Lake, then go up the same trail 750 feet in 1.1 miles to a spur trail that leads 0.4 mile to the PCT (6560). Now on the PCT, go SW 0.5 mile up to a conspicuous saddle (6870), then turn N 1.1 mile to the high point (7180) of Section Q. Continue N 1.7 miles down to the Shackleford Creek Trail (6590). Go NW

George on the PCT at Etna Summit

on the PCT 4.2 miles to the Marble Rim Trail and the Big Elk Lake Trail (6232). Still on the PCT, go N 1.0 mile down to the Canyon Creek Trail (5700), where you depart the PCT. Follow the Canyon Creek Trail 4.0 miles to the Lovers Camp TH.

Lovers Camp TH. From the 4WD road near Kidder Creek TH, retrace your route to the junction of Quartz Valley Road and First St. in the village of Greenview. Turn left (W) on Quartz Valley Road and go 9.2 miles through the village of Mugginsville and across Meamber Bridge to Scott River Road. Turn left (W) on Scott River Road and go 6.9 miles to paved FR 44N45. Turn left (SW)—follow signs for Lover's Camp—and go 5.4 miles to the junction of FR 44N45 and FR 43N45. (This junction will be important in getting to the end of the next hike, Hike 3.) Stay on paved FR 43N45—follow the sign for Lovers Camp—and go 1.8 miles to the Lovers CG and TH.

Hike 3—Lovers Camp TH to Paradise TH

PCT: 5.1 miles
Hike: 10.9 miles
Map: Q-3 (Klamath NF)
Difficulty: Moderate

Hike. From Lovers Camp, hike 4.0 miles up the Canyon Creek Trail to the PCT (5700). Wind your way N 5.1 miles to the Rye Patch Trail

(6190), where you depart the PCT. Follow the Rye Patch Trail E 1.8 miles down to the Paradise TH on FR 44N44.

🚙 **Paradise TH.** Retrace your route from Lovers Camp 1.8 miles on paved FR 43N45 to its junction with dirt FR 44N45. Turn left (N) and go 2.4 miles to a junction with FR 44N41. Stay on FR 44N45 and go 0.9 mile to FR 44N44. Bear left (W) on FR 44N44 and go 3.5 miles to the the Paradise TH.

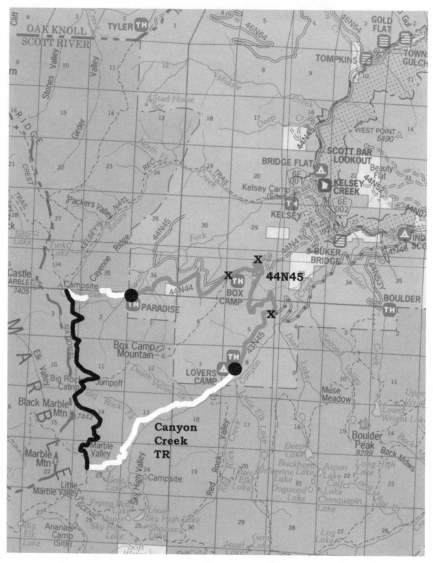

Q-3

The bridge over Grider Creek

Hike 4—Paradise TH to Grider Creek CG

PCT: 21.1 miles
Hike: 22.9 miles
Map: Q-4A and Q-4B (Klamath NF)
Difficulty: Difficult
Direction: S→N (Elevation)

Hike. (This hike is slightly longer than we usually recommend for a day hike. However, the only viable option near Huckleberry Mountain requires a great deal of walking and driving over dirt roads, some of which have serious washouts. So we have chosen a longer day hike in this region.)

From the Paradise TH (see above), hike up the Rye Patch Trail 1.8 miles to Paradise Lake (6130). Go N 1.8 miles to the Bear Lake/Turk Lake trail (6580). Continue NW 4.0 miles along the crest to Buckhorn Spring (6570). In 1.3 miles you intersect the Huckleberry Mountain Trail (6020). You then cross several logging roads in the next 6.4 miles as you descend to Road 46N72 (3200) near Cold Spring creek. From here it is 0.8 mile to a footbridge over Grider Creek (2870), which you then follow pleasantly 6.8 miles down to the Grider Creek CG (1700).

Walker Creek Road near Grider Creek CG—shortest route. From the Paradise TH, retrace your route to Scott River Road. Go west about 3 miles on Scott River Road to the Bridge CG. (This road was closed when

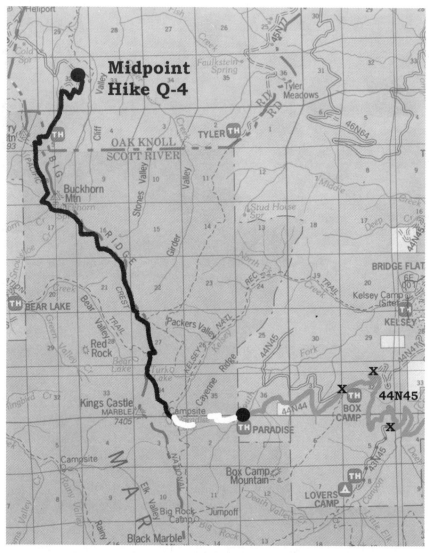

Q-4A

we field-checked it; hence, we only estimate the mileage to the Bridge CG.) From the Bridge CG, go N 13.7 miles on Scott River Road (7F01) to Scott Bar Guard Station. Continue N on 7F01 to Highway 96. Turn left (W) and go 9.5 miles to Walker Creek Road. From here, follow the directions to the Grider Creek CG below.

🚐 **Walker Creek Road near Grider Creek CG—optional route**. (If Scott River Road to Seiad Valley is still closed, use this option.) From the Paradise TH, retrace your route to the junction of Scott River Road and Quartz Valley Road near Meamber Bridge. Go E 7.0 miles on Scott River

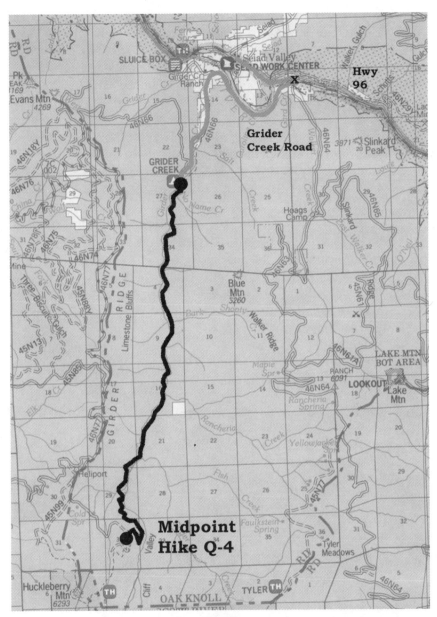

Q-4B

Road to Highway 3 in Fort Jones. Turn left (N) on Highway 3 and go 15.2 miles to an unsigned intersection just past Wal-Mart in Yreka—there are a Shell Station and McDonald's on the east side of the road. Continue N 2.6 miles on Highway 3 to Highway 263. Continue straight (N), now on Highway 263, and go 8.0 miles to Highway 96. Turn left (W) on Highway 96 and go 42.8 miles to Walker Creek Road.

🚙 **Grider Creek CG from Walker Creek Road**. From Highway 96, turn left (S) and go 50 yards on Walker Creek Road. Make an immediate right (W) onto paved Grider Road—follow the sign for the Grider Creek CG. In 2.4 miles, the pavement ends at the junction of a private road and dirt FR 46N66. Go 2.4 miles on FR 46N66 to the Grider Creek CG entrance, then 0.2 mile into the CG.

Hike 5—Grider Creek CG to Seiad Valley

PCT: 6.5 miles
Hike: 6.5 miles
Map: Q-5 (Klamath NF)

🚶 **Hike.** From the Grider Creek CG (1700), the PCT follows the road 6.5 miles into Seiad Valley. It goes along Grider Creek 2.6 miles, then along the Klamath River 2.4 miles to Highway 96 (1435), where it turns west to follow Highway 96 1.5 miles into Seiad Valley. Many people may not do this hike because of its all-road nature. We simply jogged it, one of the few places along the PCT where you can jog.

🚙 **Seiad Valley PO**. From the Grider CG, retrace your route to Highway 96. Turn left (W) on Highway 96 and go 1.5 miles to the post office and general store in the center of Seiad Valley.

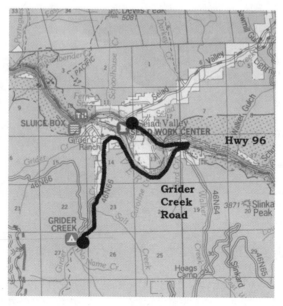

Q-5

Seiad Valley to Interstate 5 near Siskiyou Pass

Overview

PCT: 64.5 miles
Hikes (4): 64.5 miles
Declination: 17.25° E

This section of the PCT includes two day hikes in southern Oregon. We do this to maintain consistency with the Schaffer guide, Section R, which begins in Seiad Valley and ends at Highway I-5 near Siskiyou Pass in Oregon.

The California-Oregon border on the PCT was not marked by any road junctions, so we chose Wards Fork Gap as the place to end California day

Donomore Meadow from NFR 2025 near the CA-OR border

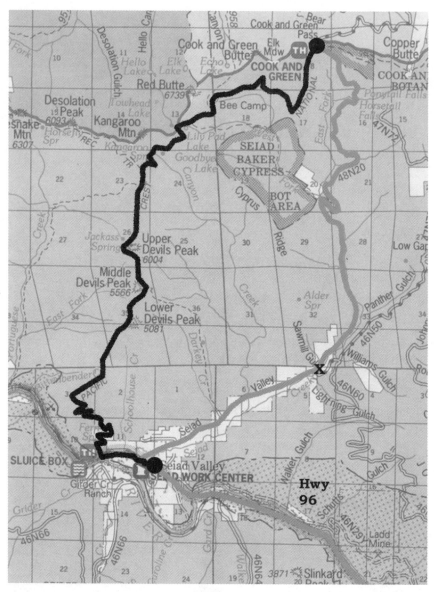

R-1

hikes and begin Oregon day hikes. Six roads converge at Wards Fork Gap—FR 1065 to Upper Applegate, two threads of FR 40S01, FR 47N01 to Klamath River, FR 48N16, and FR 48N15 to Klamath River—as do the north and south threads of the PCT.

(If you are interested, the California-Oregon border is on FR 2025, 0.5 mile north of the junction of FR 2025 and FR 40S01. It is denoted by a post along the north side of the road with the letters CALIF on one side and ORE on the other.

From the valley floor (1371), you climb over 4400 feet back to the crest, then stay on it as you go north, then east, past several minor peaks. After passing Mt. Ashland, you begin a long descent to the end of the Mt. Ashland road (4240) near Siskiyou Pass. On your easterly traverse across southern Oregon, you parallel FR 20 for some 25 miles. This makes many different day hikes possible in a very pretty setting.

Hike 1—Seiad Valley to Cook and Green Pass

PCT: 15.1 miles
Hike: 15.1 miles
Map: R-1 (Klamath NF)
Difficulty: Moderate
Direction: N→S (Elevation)

🚶 **Hike.** Hike W 0.8 mile on Highway 96, then N 5.7 miles up a ridge between Portuguese Creek and Canyon Creek to Lower Devils Peak saddle (5020). Continue N 3.9 miles to Kangaroo Springs (5760). Turn NE and go 4.7 miles past tiny Lily Pad and Echo lakes to Cook and Green Pass (4770).

🚐 **Seiad Valley PO.** From the Grider CG, where you began the last hike in Section Q, retrace your route to Highway 96. Turn left (W) and go 1.5 miles to the post office and general store in the center of Seiad Valley.

🚐 **Cook and Green Pass.** From the post office in Seiad Valley, go W 0.1 mile on Highway 96 to paved Seiad Valley Road. Turn right (NE) and go 4.0 miles to where the pavement ends and FR 48N20 begins. Continue N 8.1 miles on FR 48N20 to Cook and Green Pass.

Hike 2—Cook and Green Pass to Wards Fork Gap

PCT: 18.8 miles
Hike: 18.8 miles
Map: R-2A and R-2B (Klamath NF)
Difficulty: Moderate

🚶 **Hike.** From Cook and Green Pass, hike E 2.8 miles to Trail 11W02 (6080), then 2.2 miles to Horse Creek Trail 11W01 (6040). Continue E 4.7 miles to where the PCT touches FR 47N81, then parallel that road 3.1 miles to pass a spur trail (6630) near Buckhorn Camp. Here, veer NE and parallel FR 40S01 as you hike 6.0 miles to Wards Fork Gap (5317).

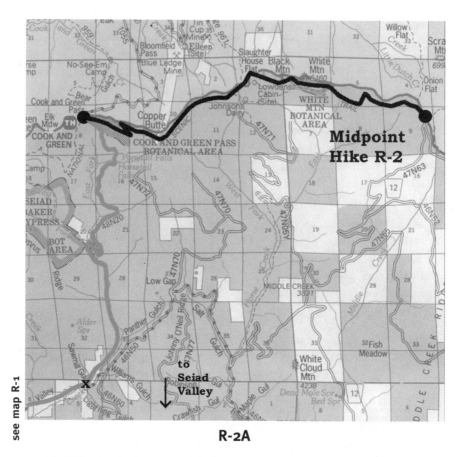

R-2A

🚗 **Wards Fork Gap—from Cook and Green Pass**. Retrace your route to the post office in Seiad Valley. Turn left (E) on Highway 96 and go 27.8 miles to paved Beaver Creek Road (FR 11). Turn left (N)—follow the WARDS FORK 22 sign—and go 5.5 miles to dirt FR 47N01. Bear left (NW) on FR 47N01 and go 3.2 miles to the junction of FR 47N01 and 48N15. Bear right (N)—follow the WARDS FORK sign—on FR 48N15 and go 1.2 miles to an unsigned junction. Bear right (NW) and go up 5.6 miles to Wards Fork Gap.

🚗 **Wards Fork Gap—from Siskiyou Gap in Oregon**. From Siskiyou Gap, go W 7.8 miles on FR 20 to FR 2025. Turn left (S) and go 5.2 miles to FR 40S01. (The road stays the same, but the road signs change as you move from one National Forest jurisdiction to another.) Continue straight (S) on FR 40S01 and go 1.8 miles to the junction of FR 40S01 and FR 48N14Y. Continue south on FR 40S01 1.2 miles to Wards Fork Gap.

see map R-3

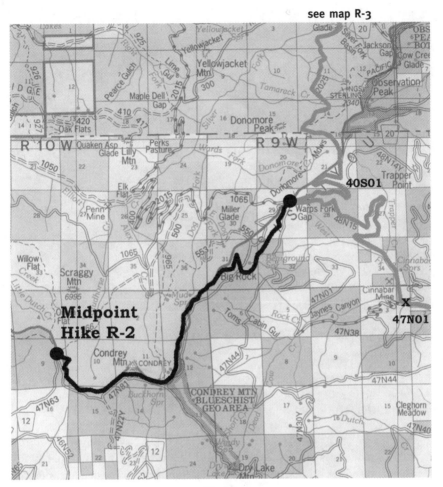

R-2B

Old corral at Wrangle CG near Wrangle Gap

Hike 3—Wards Fork Gap to Siskiyou Gap

PCT: 13.3 miles
Hike: 13.3 miles
Map: R-3 (Rogue River NF)
Difficulty: Moderate

Hike. From Wards Fork Gap (5317) hike N 2.9 miles through Donomore Meadows to FR 2025. (We did this hike in May; we met hail, snow, and howling winds.) Continue NE 4.0 miles past Observation Peak and Observation Gap on your way to Jackson Gap (7040). Now, parallel FR 20 for 2.6 miles to Wrangle Gap (6496). Still staying near FR 20, you hike 3.8 miles around Red Mountain and on to Siskiyou Gap (5890).

(Because the PCT closely follows FR 20 in this area, you can use it to easily show others parts of the PCT. You can plan short hikes with spectacular scenery, or longer ones for the more adventurous. This stretch is similar to the PCT in the Mt. Laguna region near San Diego in southern California, where the PCT parallels Highway S1, and where we have done many short and long day hikes.)

Siskiyou Gap—from Wards Fork Gap. From Wards Fork Gap, go NE 1.2 miles on FR 40S01—follow the sign for Mt. Ashland—to the junction of 40S01 and 48N14Y. Bear left (W)—stay on FR 40S01—and go 1.8 miles to the junction of FR 40S01 and FR 2025. (The road designations change here due to a change in National Forest jurisdictions). Bear left (N) on FR 2025—follow the sign for Silver Fork Gap—and go 0.5 mile to

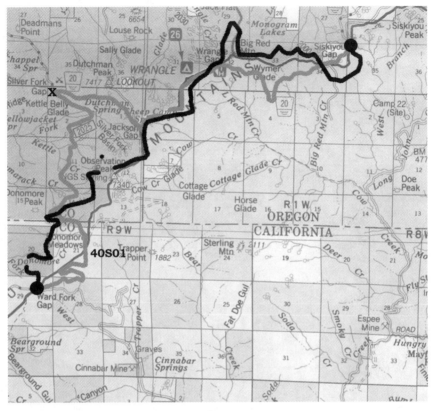

R-3

the CALIF/ORE border sign. Go up another 0.6 mile to the PCT as it comes out of Donomore Meadows. Now, continue straight (N) and go 4.1 miles on FR 2025 to FR 20. Turn right (E) on FR 20 and go 7.8 miles to Siskiyou Gap.

🚗 **Siskiyou Gap—from I-5 near Mt. Ashland Road**. From the junction of FR 20 (Mt. Ashland road) and Old Siskiyou road near Exit 6 (Mt. Ashland) off Highway I-5, go W 9.1 miles on paved Mt. Ashland road past the ski lifts to where the pavement ends and FR 20 begins. Go W 7.6 miles on FR 20 to Siskiyou Gap.

Hike 4—Siskiyou Gap to Highway I-5 near Siskiyou Pass

PCT: 17.3 miles
Hike: 17.3 miles
Map: R-4 (Rogue River NF)
Difficulty: Moderate

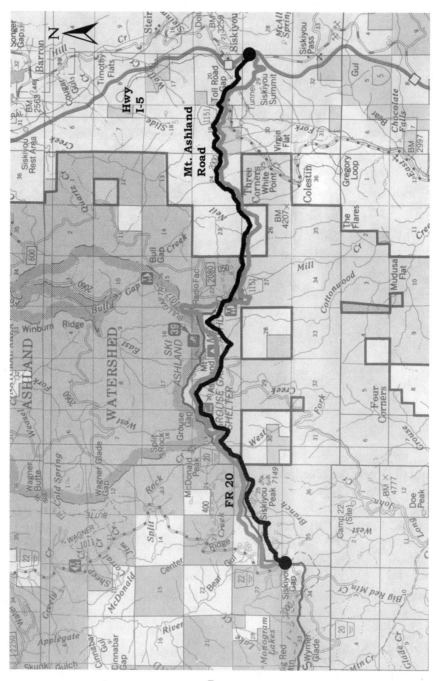

R-4

🥾 **Hike**. From Siskiyou Gap (5890), you parallel FR 20 as you hike E 1.6 miles to Long John Saddle (5880), then 5.0 miles to Grouse Gap (6630). In another 3.4 miles, you cross FR 20 east of the Mt. Ashland ski area. Now, begin your 7.3 miles down to the end of Mt. Ashland road at Old Siskiyou road.

🚗 **Highway I-5 near Siskiyou Pass**. From Siskiyou Gap, go E 7.6 miles on FR 20 to where the pavement and Mt. Ashland Road begin. Follow Mt. Ashland Road past the ski lifts and go down 9.1 miles to Old Siskiyou Road near Exit 6 (Mt. Ashland) off Highway I-5. From this junction, the southbound PCT TH is 0.1 mile north along Old Siskiyou road and the northbound PCT is 0.4 mile south along Old Siskiyou road. The trail follows Old Siskiyou road between these two THs, both of which are clearly marked. The best place to park is the large dirt lot directly across from Mt. Ashland road.

The PCT crosses a field along FR 20 near Grouse Gap

INDEX

Boldface denotes maps.